Evidence-Based Investing

EVIDENCE-BASED Investing

Maximize Returns Using the **Methods Proved** to **Really Work**

GRAHAM SOMMER

Contents

Summary: A detailed system for personal investment based on proven techniques is presented. This book shows how online stock index trend analysis, applied to stock index fund investing, has increased rates of return by at least 6.2 to 9.4% per year.

Library of Congress Cataloging-in-Publication Data:
Graham Sommer
Title: Evidence Based Investing
ISBN: 13-978-0-615-37348-5
1. Index Funds 2. Investments

Design by Katy Brown
Index by Nancy Humphreys
Project editor Melissa Moore

Printed in the United States of America

First Printing: October 2010

Foreword

For some years, I have worked to develop an investing scheme that is both practical and useful. I have felt that an investing system, to be truly practical, would have to be easily implemented by an individual investor who has little time to set up and monitor an investment portfolio. To be useful, the system would have to provide returns superior to those available with standard investing techniques, while limiting risk to acceptable levels.

The motivation for my efforts has come both from the need to invest both my personal funds, which have become more substantial over the years, and a desire to provide assistance to family members, friends, and acquaintances who have expressed some anxiety related to their unfamiliarity with investing. As my responsibilities and capital have increased, I had no other option than to become interested and involved in investment techniques. I have done my best to develop a system that works as I propose, and it has worked very well for me for some years.

It became evident, though, that I would need to write it down in some detail for it to be of genuine assistance to others. Even though I have kept things as simple as possible, it is not easy to quickly go over verbally the details of the system, nor to provide its logical and historical justifications. I could not expect others to accept my guidance until I wrote down and made very clear the basis for my approach.

If we hope to invest successfully and to secure our financial futures, we really need an organized, systematic approach; this is more important than ever in this time of turmoil and severe declines in world markets. Over the past year, the world financial crisis has lead to severe losses in the large majority of accounts. This has occurred at a particularly bad time for a great many baby boomers approaching retirement. An effective investment strategy is particularly important at the present time, since we all have been given unprecedented responsibility for our personal investments in 401(k) and other retirement accounts, as well as taxable investments.

In order to define a system that met my goals I have had to address investing dogma in a couple of forms; I'll call them the old dogma and the new. Standard investing techniques have long involved hiring financial advisors, who then would create a stock-and-bond portfolio. This was the old dogma of personal investing: invest via an advisor who will manage your money for you. If you look more closely at this model, however, you'll find that the high fees charged by such advisors have been very damaging to clients' rates of return. The approach to outperforming the market by stock selection (stock picking) has been proved futile in recent years by virtually every objective study.

In the last three decades, we've seen the emergence of the low-fee stock index fund initiated by John Bogle and others. The superiority of employing such funds rather than taking the high-fee stock selection approach of the past has been made clearly manifest in many rigorous comparisons. The approach to investing among many knowledgeable investors today is to invest solely via such stock index funds, with bonds and bond funds making up the fixed-income portion of a portfolio. Although today's ongoing market turmoil is seen as a source of vexation, a common view among knowledgeable investors today is that the most viable approach to investing is via a stock index fund/bond portfolio that will basically remain fixed (with occasional rebalancing) indefinitely. This might be called the new dogma of personal investing.

A near-universal tenet of both the old and new dogmas is that market timing—to take advantage of uptrends while limiting losses in downtrends—is impossible. When one looks at the history of efforts to perform such timing, it is not difficult to understand this general perception. If you can't use either stock selection or market timing to improve performance, though, there seems really no alternative to the index fund/bond buy-and-hold strategy. No advantage over the overall market seems possible.

If one investigates the problem further, however, it becomes evident that major modern U.S. and foreign index funds have characteristics that make their longer-term movements very amenable to useful analysis by trend-following techniques. The relatively low volatility and constant stock composition of major stock indices allows computer-based trend analysis to gain a substantial edge over the general market. A rather straightforward approach using online data and analysis tools, to be described in this book, has allowed enhancement of rates of return from 6.2% to 9.4% per annum compared to buy-and-hold, since 1995. The system would have kept one completely out of the crashing world markets in 2008.

Modern low-fee mutual funds, in concert with powerful online tools for analyzing market movements, can be exploited to substantially increase your rate of return on investments. With some effort to organize and monitor your investments in this way, you can readily learn and apply techniques to greatly improve your personal investing results.

Acknowledgments

I have appreciated very much the support and suggestions of a number of friends with whom I discussed the possibility of writing this book. Early on, I was greatly encouraged by the comments and suggestions of David Hayes and Steve and Elisabetta Bigsby. Bob Smiley offered very useful suggestions concerning the literature on the performance of mutual fund investing. Kate Spelman and Sophie Cohen have very helpfully guided me through many of the mysteries of manuscript preparation and publication.

I have been greatly aided by two good friends who have reviewed the manuscript at various stages, and offered many suggestions that have been extremely helpful. Jack MacDonald's careful review and ideas were really appreciated, and resulted in an updated manuscript that is much enhanced. I am particularly grateful for the very enthusiastic support and many ideas (almost all of which are present in the final product) from Eric Olcott. Eric's support and many creative suggestions have really helped me, and made the whole process of writing the book a lot more fun.

CHAPTER 1

THE PURPOSE OF THE BOOK

Over the years, I've developed a system for personal investment that has enjoyed considerable success. The major reason I undertook this book was a desire to explain the investment approach I have been using for some time to friends and family. While I haven't made a practice of volunteering advice, conversations on investing do tend to come up, and there has been interest in my approach, which I have tried to address by writing it down. Along with interest, there has been some skepticism, particularly concerning the possibility of market timing. I don't think I can expect anybody to take my system very seriously unless it is well documented, so I will provide an explanation of the reasoning behind this system, and outline the record of historical success supporting it. In addition to stating what I am doing and why, I am providing my take on several fundamental principles of investing.

Personal Investing Is Too Important Not to Take an Interest

It seems in the modern era we are increasingly being forced to make the important investment decisions that will largely determine the future financial courses of our lives, yet we often do not feel prepared for this responsibility. To a considerable extent, this increased need for self-direction of our investments is the result of the shift of company retirement plans from defined-benefit plans, in which funds targeted for retirement funding are invested professionally, to largely self-directed plans such as IRA, 401(k), and related plans. The desirability of this new structure, requiring self-directed investing for retirement, is questionable, since the average person has little knowledge of this field. Nevertheless, the large majority of us have to deal increasingly with the present situation, and manage as best we can our retirement savings plans and any taxable accounts we control.

In my discussions with friends and colleagues about self-direction of investments, I've encountered quite a bit of resistance to the concept of taking an active role in individual investment efforts, and a widespread feeling that personal investment is beyond the capability of the average person. It is my general philosophy in life, in fact, to "leave it to the experts" in the vast majority of areas. If there is a problem with the car, or something to fix around the house, or a problem with my computer I can't readily handle, I will always call on and pay someone with real expertise to do the job. I have found by experience that this is almost always the faster, more effective, and, ultimately, cheaper approach. While the average person may perceive a lack of investment expertise, they also may have a feeling that an active role in personal investing will be inordinately time-consuming, and they may have little interest in spending available time directing investments.

While you can claim ignorance and/or lack of time to deal with investments, these are not wise approaches; too much is at stake. The knowledge required for superior investment performance is really not very complicated, and can be mastered with just a little time and effort. With any reasonable degree of organization on your part, the time spent on a more active approach to investing will not be much greater than that required by passive participation, but the rewards are likely to be improved considerably.

When considered fully, the lack-of-knowledge and lack-of-time arguments don't really hold up. As to time, most of us put a great deal of effort into shopping around to find the lowest possible prices for purchases—we spend many hours shopping for the lowest airfare or the cheapest price for a pair of shoes. While frugality is commendable, we might consider the use of our time here as that required to manage our investment possibilities. In the time it takes to find a $20 saving on a pair of shoes, we might be able to take some simple steps to enhance our investment performance by many thousands of dollars.

There is a great inconsistency in working hard all your life and saving money, and then having little involvement in protecting and growing those earnings through investment. The money you are directing in your retirement instruments or taxable accounts is the tangible reward for many years of your daily labors and saving. We've worked very hard to make this money and save it, and it is both unwise and inconsistent to not devote at least some effort into its direction. If you keep your investment strategy as simple as possible, which is quite easy in the modern age, it will not be difficult to invest successfully without undue effort or attention on your part.

It is important to understand the important innovations in personal investing in recent years, such as low-fee stock index funds and bond funds, and the invaluable online tools for investment management and trading. With these new tools, effective investing can be performed very readily, and self-direction of investment is truly practical. Even if you choose to invest in a more traditional fashion through a broker or advisor, you will find that knowledge of basic investment principles is a great boon. Much of the mystery surrounding investment may fall away, and you will be able to deal with any financial advisor much more effectively.

The Basic Strategy

There are several basic principles of the system I have developed and propose for your consideration, and the reasoning behind each of these will be explained in later chapters. The strategy concerns the direction of an account comprising only the standard investment vehicles of stocks and bonds held in mutual funds. This basic approach seems appropriate for a system intended to be of value for personal investing in either taxable accounts or retirement vehicles such as 401(k) accounts. While other forms of investment are often considered, including real estate, commodities, and gold, it is more difficult to invest directly in these entities through standard markets.

The above considerations lead me to state the bedrock principle of my investment strategy, which is to *keep everything as simple as possible* while achieving good rates of return with acceptable risk. Any system that requires a great deal of time and effort to implement will simply not be followed over the long term by the average investor, and will fall under its own weight.

In addition to describing the mechanics of the system of investment I propose, while keeping it as simple as possible, I will provide background and evidence supporting its use. I will scarcely be comprehensive in my discussion of background, but will present only the information required. I believe that the evidence I will provide on the superior investment performance attainable with the techniques I propose will convince you of their utility and practicality. I will reference recent books and articles that cover many basic topics much more fully, and can provide more background information to the reader if desired.

Learning from History

It is important to look at the history of markets and investing in designing an effective approach to personal investment. While the course of future markets is always cloudy, the most likely future scenarios can be anticipated to a large extent by interpreting historic data in the context of present-day economic and market realities. As to the history of markets, much can be learned from patterns in the economy and market movements that reveal, on close examination, features that repeat at rather regular cycles over the years. These recurring features, changes in their characteristics over time, and their relevance to analysis of present-day markets will be stressed in this book, and illustrated with real historic data.

It is only by the determination of the characteristics of investment techniques that have proved successful in the past that we can design a strategy with a realistic chance for superior performance in the future. The only reasonable basis for an investing strategy would seem to be careful examination of the evidence as to which techniques have worked best in the past, and to use in the future only those found most effective.

Throughout the book, I will do my best to carefully document which investment techniques have been most effective in the past. I'll follow this with recommendations for an investment approach based on the historical record; I'll call this approach evidence-based investing.

In addition to overall market history, I've certainly considered my own personal investment history in determining what I feel is the best strategy for individual investment. In particular, there are a number of features of my investment approach in the past that I now view as mistakes—errors from which I have learned a great deal, on reflection. While you may have benefited from your own investing experience, perhaps you can benefit from some of mine as well.

One error was my effort to invest in individual stocks through my analysis of the best information I was able to find. Although this approach might seem eminently reasonable, and is still the basis of most investment portfolios under management, the results attained were mediocre; clearly the time spent had not lead to superior performance. Although in the past, I felt that my analysis of individual stocks might lead to superior returns, I will present a great deal of evidence supporting the general futility of this approach, and the superiority of simply investing in U.S. and major international stock index funds.

In the past, I have delegated funds to investment professionals paid substantial fees to manage without my direct involvement. In the end, I found that the enhancement of returns resulting from the management was not significant, but that the long-term effects of fees led to a significant decrease in my returns. This book will evaluate carefully the available evidence on the records of investment performance of professional money managers, and the effects of the fees charged. Clear documentation of the mediocrity of returns generally achieved by professional managers charging relatively high fees has lead me to deal exclusively with large, low-fee entities.

Whereas I used to believe that there was really no alternative to a buy-and-hold approach to investment, it has also become evident to me that yet another mistake was the maintenance of such a strategy when it had clearly outlived its usefulness. For almost the whole of the two decades from 1980 until 2000, a buy-and-hold strategy worked very well, since the United States and most world markets simply saw a continuing bull market year after year without significant reversal. The market turbulence beginning with the very damaging bear markets of 2000 through 2002 has made it clear that the buy-and-hold strategy for stocks no longer provides satisfactory returns. To deal with such markets, it has become necessary to develop a system for timing the long-term trends of major market stock indices, and their corresponding index mutual funds. The system developed has proved very beneficial in recent years, and I will detail it fully in this book.

While none of the conventional approaches described above may appear to represent serious errors, the narrative of this book is based around the startling deficiencies of these rather standard methods. An alternative investment strategy to standard techniques will be presented in detail, and the historical evidence clearly demonstrating its superiority will be described. The system is a practical one that can be readily implemented by the average investor.

An Integrated System that Works

Many of the features of the system for personal investing I've adopted are hardly original. The advantages of investing in stocks via low-fee stock index funds have been put forward in recent years by a number of authors[1]. What is original about my approach is the integration of the low-fee index and bond funds concept along with an effective method of market timing that has proved particularly useful in application to trading between stock index mutual funds and bond funds.

With a bit of organization and planning, I believe it likely that a system similar to that which I will propose can, in whole or in part, become a powerful and effective approach for your personal investing.

CHAPTER 2

THE OLD INVESTING . . . AND THE NEW

While the world of investing has been rather static in principle for a great many years, relatively recent innovation in the tools available for personal investment have created remarkable opportunities. The creation of low-fee index mutual funds and online tools for managing and researching personal investments has greatly improved the prospects for the savvy investor to enhance both the control and profitability of their investments. The older model of relying on a "full-service" stockbroker or other agent who charges substantial fees to assemble a stock-and-bond portfolio is receding in importance.

Elements of the W$W world, as described in the sidebar, are still with us today, but they are becoming less prominent as more investors avail themselves of the much greater range of investment information and much lower fees available today. Decisions on stock purchases in that era would be made using a full-service broker similar to most of the panelists and many of the guests on W$W. The purchase of a stock or bond was a significant commitment, since the fees for such a transaction could run to

THE WORLD OF WALL $TREET WEEK

Many of you may recall Wall $treet Week (W$W) with the iconic Louis Rukeyser, the long-running investment news and information TV program that ran in its original form from 1970 until 2002 [1]. I used to watch it many Fridays at 7:30 PM, and was taken with this window into the financial world. The program was extremely popular for an investing show, and the program material seemed quite state-of-the-art. In retrospect, the show now seems like a microcosm of the particular style of investing in those days.

The format of the show was set early on, and changed very little over the years; Lou, always immaculately attired, and would begin with a summary on the week's financial news, followed by a summary of stock market trends and statistics. This was generally followed by a look at the current status of a basket of technical market indicators used to derive a "Wall $treet Week Index," initially developed by analyst Robert Nurock.

Following Lou's introduction, he moderated a panel discussion with colleagues, most of whom were stockbrokers (well-dressed, but not as well as Lou) of the full-service variety. The panelists then answered a number of questions mailed in by viewers, and a guest was introduced by Lou, leading to a discussion with the panel members. Typically, the guest would be an analyst of a stock sector who would discuss the prospects for that particular sector of the market. The emphasis was always on providing names of the stocks best positioned for future market success; "Do any of these stocks have names?" Lou would often ask.

And then there was an annual New Year's show where some of Lou's stalwart colleagues would dress up in tuxedos and suggest a portfolio of stocks for the next year and an expected general market range. Kudos were awarded to whoever had done the best job of stock selection over the past year.

When 7:30 PM on Fridays rolls around, many of us who are interested in the stock market miss W$W, and wish there were a newer weekly version of the program on the air now. It will take a modern version of someone with the acumen, wit, and panache of Lou Rukeyser to pull it off.

several percentage points of the cash value of the transaction. There was an implicit view that the combination of the top-notch information and superior analytic capabilities of the broker and the research division at his or her firm would very likely provide superior returns over time.

The New World of Investment

While I did enjoy W$W and learned quite a bit from the show over the years, I can see now that there were a few deficiencies that could have been better addressed. For example, I don't recall any significant discussion of bedrock investment principles such as diversification, or the allocation of assets in an orderly manner. The very serious impact of high transaction costs (discussed in Chapter 5) was never mentioned, at least when I was watching. Perhaps this is not unexpected, given the preponderance of "full-fee" brokers as panelists on the show.

This traditional approach is passing, and newer and more efficient approaches are clearly evident today. These newer approaches are not yet fully realized, but their outlines seem clear. Let me elaborate.

The approaches of the earlier era were almost entirely concerned with the creation of a portfolio of selected stocks as investment vehicles, and the overriding concept was that skillful stock picking was the critical element to any investment strategy. In more recent years, however, it has been clearly shown that excellent diversification, minimization of taxation, and superior long-term performance can be achieved much more simply by using low-fee stock index mutual funds. Since the creation of the first index mutual fund in 1975, based on the Standard & Poor's (S&P) 500 average, it has become increasingly evident that one can attain consistently better results through such low-fee vehicles[2] than with the traditional stock-picker approach. The overwhelming evidence of the superiority of this approach will be summarized in Chapter 4.

Whereas in the old world of investing stock trades were performed by brokers charging exorbitant fees, investors are now clearly benefiting from the robust competition among discount brokers. Securities transaction fees charged by discount brokers are a small fraction of the prior fee structure. Minimal or absent fees are now featured in trading among the mutual funds in taxable or 401(k) accounts. There really is a whole new world of fee minimization in trading today from which an individual investor can benefit, if one knows where to look.

The growth of the Internet has provided revolutionary new tools for personal investing, for those capable of exploiting its possibilities. The fees charged for online transactions are typically even lower than those arranged otherwise. The convenience of having current account information available and trading electronically on your home computer with 24/7 access represent huge advances. There are limitless online opportunities for research on stocks, markets, and funds today, and there is little need to rely on a broker or other agent for information relevant to investment. The type of information that was in the past only available through research divisions of major investment houses is now freely accessible through your online fund or brokerage site.

A great many websites are also available today that offer free access to sophisticated online tools for technical analysis of stocks and market indices. The contribution of technical analysis and market timing techniques were not accorded much credence in the world of W$W, and still have little place in the conventional investment doctrine of today. In Chapters 8 through 11, however, trading methods are outlined in which online charting and analysis techniques using Internet tools have allowed markedly superior returns in trading major stock index mutual funds compared to a buy-and-hold strategy. I will be endeavoring to convince you that this online capability has great potential in an integrated plan of personal investment based on stock index mutual funds and bond mutual funds.

We are actually not wholly in a "new" post-W$W world by any means, but in a transitional period. Many of the features of the W$W world now coexist with the remarkable current innovations in the tools of investing. There are still plenty of investors, for example, who may never go near a computer in their investing efforts, but rely solely on full-fee brokers for their guidance, and the performance of trades in individual stocks. Their numbers continue to diminish, however, and those who wish to excel in their investment performance in the future will be well advised to learn how to exploit the many new opportunities now available.

CHAPTER 3

THE OLD RETIREMENT... AND THE NEW

Having sufficient funds to live well during the retirement years is clearly a major goal of a saving and investment program. In the last chapter, a number of the features of the new investment strategy were outlined, and it is quite clear that there is an ongoing revolution in the mechanics of investing, with very clear benefits of the newer features to the knowledgeable investor.

Similarly, in my lifetime there has been an accompanying revolution in the financial mechanics of retirement in the United States; unfortunately, the changes in this important area do not appear so uniformly beneficial to U.S. workers. The changes have primarily been dictated by the perceived need of companies and institutions to reduce costs in an increasingly competitive and globalized world.

The new retirement paradigm shifts responsibility from companies and institutions to individuals, and is highly dependent on instruments not even designed to fully support individuals in retirement. The change in retirement models from the classic company pension, or defined benefit

(DB) plan, to the defined contribution (DC) model has been dramatic. In 1983, 62% of U.S. workers had a traditional DB pension plan only, whereas only 12% had 401(k)s. In 2009, about 20% have a traditional DB pension and about two-thirds have only 401(k)s[1].

How Much Will I Need?

For any worker in America, the first questions concerning retirement should be how much you should be saving, and how much will be required in retirement. While these questions perhaps seems obvious, many workers might not get around to making these determinations. There are many easy-to-use tools, again online, that you can use to estimate how much will be required. If you do a web search on "retirement calculator," you'll be presented with a large number of rather sophisticated online calculators that can readily assist. A number of inputs are requested, and estimates of how much you should be saving, and the capability of replacement of a certain percentage of preretirement income can be calculated. I rather like the calculator provided by Fidelity Investments (Figure 3-1).

The calculation of the amount of capital that must be saved to generate a continuing, real (inflation-adjusted) withdrawal of funds for many years is complex one, in which assumptions must be made concerning rates of return, inflation, and so on. In one assessment of this problem[2], it was shown that for withdrawal of $50,000 per year for a period of 20 to 25 years, $1 million of capital would be required. When the calculations are done rigorously, it is likely surprising just how much capital is really required at the time of retirement.

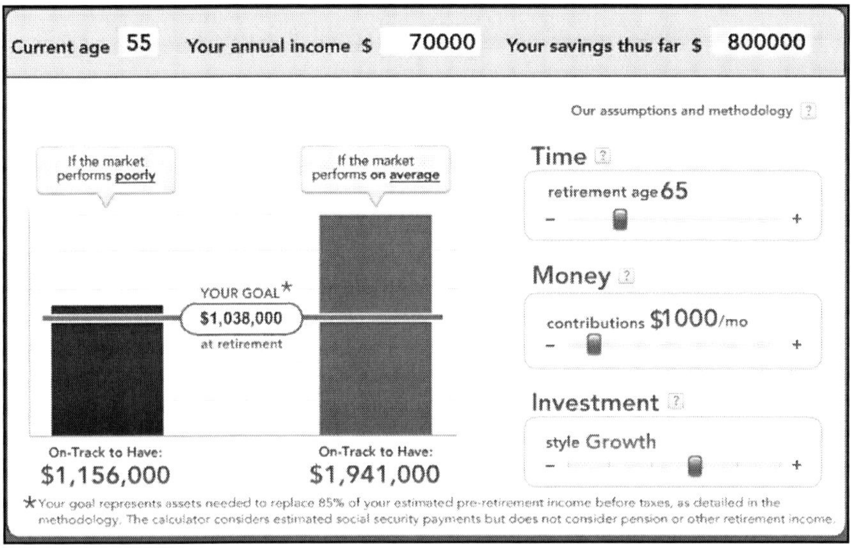

Figure 3-1: Sample output from the Fidelity retirement calculator: From the inputs shown at the top and right, the assets at the time of retirement needed to provide 85% of preretirement income are calculated in this example. By changing variables, calculations can be made that reflect any desired conditions.

Source: Fidelity Online Retirement Tools (http://personal.fidelity.com/planning/retirement/content/myPlan/index.shtml)

The Investment Vehicles Used to Fund Retirement

Having some knowledge concerning how much savings will be required, it then seems reasonable to consider the vehicles available for an individual in the United States to use for actually saving money in a regular way. In addition to regular taxable savings accounts, future retirement income can come from Social Security, and tax-sheltered IRA- and 401(k)-type plans. These sources have variable potential to provide substantial retirement income for an individual. While a highly successful program, the Social Security program was never designed as a sole retirement vehicle but as a supplement.

Of the possibilities for tax-sheltered investment, the 401(k)-type plans are potentially the most important, since you can use them to save much more than with IRAs, often with substantial "free" matching funds provided by an employer. The 401(k) world also includes the 403(b) plans for educational institutions, and the 457 plans for government employees, but I will refer to all these as 401(k) plans.

These plans were not initially set up as anything like comprehensive retirement solutions, but as vehicles to allow highly paid executives to shelter retirement savings pretax in 1980[3]. They evolved into an extremely popular retirement approach in the United States when it became clear that the 401(k) mechanism would allow workers to shelter substantial funds that could remain untaxed until retirement. Companies and institutions have switched from DB plans to the DC 401(k) plans, since their costs are far lower. Importantly, the switch from DB to 401(k) shifts from the company to the individual the responsibility and opportunity for saving, investing, and planning for retirement.

Some Problems with the New Approach

In spite of the ubiquity of 401(k) plans as the basis for modern retirement planning, there are a number of significant problems with a mechanism not really designed to function as the mainstay of retirement funding of the population.

1. At any given time, only about half of the U.S. private sector workforce is eligible to participate in a 401(k) plan.

2. There is little standardization of such plans. The percentage of matching funds provided by companies is variable, generally from 3% to 6%[4], and (frighteningly) can be discontinued at any time by the company if it desires. The vehicles available for investment are chosen by the company and restrict investment choices undesirably. While many experts favor stock index funds, for example, there is no requirement even to offer a stock index fund as an option.

3. While employers are required to provide some level of investment guidance to employees, the 401(k) system relies on self-directed investment by individuals, many of whom have little knowledge of investing. In both Nebraska[5] and Virginia[6] (see Chapter 5, in which experiences in these two states are described), comparisons have been made between the performance of self-directed 401(k)-type programs for government workers and the performance of standard DB pension models. In both cases, the 401(k) approach proved a failure compared to DB, primarily because of the poor investment decisions of the participants.

HOW WELL HAVE 401(K) PLANS PREPARED PARTICIPANTS FOR RETIREMENT?

Compared to the lofty sums experts indicate will be needed to generate income in retirement, the amounts typically saved by 401(k) participants are quite small. For those individuals nearing retirement only 23% have saved $250,000 or more, and 28% have saved less than $10,000[7].

Only about 15 to 20% of individuals save the maximum contribution allowable, and about 25% don't participate at all in 401(k) programs for which they are eligible[8]. While experts indicate that we should have about total savings of about 10 times our annual salary in savings at the time of retirement, the total savings in the U.S. is closer to 3 times annual salary.

Perhaps we cannot expect the 401(k), which was never designed to provide retirement income as a stand-alone, to prepare the average worker better for retirement—the situation we see indicates that some more effective approach is sorely needed.

4. Participants simply are not putting enough funds into 401(k) plans to meet their requirements for retirement. To maintain their standards of living, Americans will need to save ten times their annual pay in their 401(k) plans by the time they retire. However, in a recent study, 401(k) participants near retirement had only about three times their annual pay in these plans, and this was before the market meltdown of 2008. Many 401(k) participants are in fact now continuing to work well past retirement age due simply to financial need, a situation they did not consider in their younger years[9].

The relevant bottom line here is that if you are a worker, the retirement planning ball is almost entirely in your court. It is clearly required that you play as well as possible.

While your employer, investment company, or advisor may provide some support, you will be responsible for deciding how much to save, you must have the discipline to save continuously over your working life, and you are ultimately the investment director for the funds that will support you in retirement. The latter responsibility puts a lot of weight on the shoulders of the individual, which wasn't the case in the earlier DB plan era.

I've encouraged an active interest in investing on the part of individuals, and it is pretty clear that your active and knowledgeable participation is required more now than ever before.

CHAPTER 4

INSTRUMENTS: STOCKS AND BONDS AND THEIR FUNDS

If we wish to watch our savings grow as much as possible over the years, we must have a substantial portion of our capital in stocks. The reason is that, over the years, stocks have given substantially higher overall rates of return than alternate investments such as bonds and government treasury bills, as shown in the chart below. If one looks at U.S. markets over the century since 1900, the pattern of superior returns with stocks compared to U.S. treasury bonds and bills is evident (Figure 4-1).

If stocks are the best vehicle for investing, the next major question presenting itself is the nature of our participation. Among the options are the creation of a portfolio of individual stocks, the purchase of actively managed stock mutual funds, or the use of stock index mutual funds that simply mirror the prices of certain market indices.

There is abundant solid evidence available concerning the relative merits of these options, and I will summarize some important relevant data here:

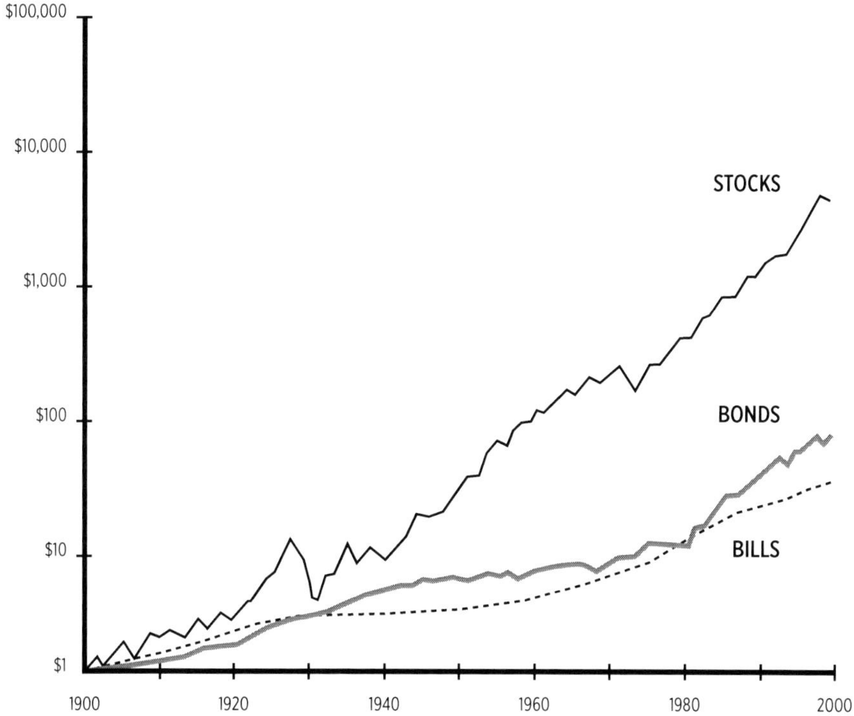

Figure 4-1: Comparative plots of the cumulative rates of return for United States stocks, treasury bonds, and treasury bills over the twentieth century.

There is more volatility, or variability, over the shorter term for stock prices compared to bonds or bills over time as shown above. Since 2000, stock returns have been relatively poor, but stocks still offer superior long-term rates of return compared to bonds and bills.

Source: Bernstein, W. 2002. *The Four Pillars of Investing*. New York: McGraw-Hill. Page 22.

THE KEY TYPES OF STOCK MUTUAL FUNDS AVAILABLE TODAY

As we will be seeing, the evidence shows that investing in stocks using stock mutual funds makes a lot more sense than creating your own portfolio of individual stocks. There a number of general types of stock mutual funds that might be considered.

Actively Managed Funds While individual stock investment has long been an option, the possibility of decreasing individual stock risk through broad stock diversification, and the potential for improved returns through professional management lead to the creation of stock mutual funds early in the twentieth century.

Initially, these funds represented a collection of stocks favored by the management of a particular fund; stocks that seemed particularly promising were purchased by management, and (often for an substantial fee) individual investors could purchase shares representing units of the favored stock collection. These funds were *actively managed*, in that the stocks in the collection represented those favored by management, who would frequently sell stocks that they felt were less promising than others, which they proceeded to buy. Thus, the mix of stocks represented by such a fund is constantly changing according to the investment decisions of management. This active approach to management is reflected in the general description of all such funds as *actively managed*.

Stock Index Funds Over the course of many years, numerous stock "indices" have been created as quantitative measures of a particular segment of the stock market. The course of the price of an index provides an often useful indication of the general course of an overall market or market sector. We are most familiar with indices such as the Dow Jones industrial average and the S&P 500 Average, which were set up to provide measures of the overall U.S. stock market. A great many stock indices have been created in recent years, representing the composite price levels of selected stocks in particular categories of U.S. stocks, or of foreign stock markets. These provide measures of the price levels in various sectors in which there is investor interest, and provide ready indications of the overall price levels in those sectors.

It was not until the 1970s that the possibility was conceived of creating stock mutual funds based not on active management in picking stocks, but on simply reflecting a selected market index. The mechanics of creating a collection of stocks that approximate closely a particular stock market average, such as the S&P 500 Average, does not afford much freedom to the manager, since all that can be done is to purchase and update a collection of stocks found in a stock average.

As will be discussed further, though, this lack of flexibility has significant advantages: the fact that little trading is required to create and maintain a stock index fund results in a number of important benefits to the purchaser, including much lower management fees, since "active" management is not involved.

CONTINUED

Exchange-Traded Funds Exchange-traded funds (ETFs) represent an even more recent innovation than stock index funds. Such funds are created to provide a vehicle for participation in a market sector in which there may be substantial investor interest. The sector can be just about any area of investment: stock sectors, stock indices, commodity prices, or very specific stock sectors such as solar power stocks. The funds differ from classical funds managed by fund companies. The shares created are purchased not from a fund company; instead, they are traded on markets like individual stocks.

While a very large number of such funds exist, their market capitalization is a small percentage of that represented by the more established actively managed and stock index funds. ETFs provide a rather new approach to investing, and may be worth consideration if you wish to participate in a particular sector that may not be represented by more conventional funds. It is important to note that many ETFs are managed so as to reflect a wide range of specific stock market indices, and thus are effectively index funds.

As we will see, a key consideration in selecting any fund will always be limiting the fees paid to fund management in order to maximize our rates of return.

1. A number of rigorous academic studies have examined the performance of actively managed funds in the United States, and drawn conclusions as to their overall performance relative to standard market indices. Some representative studies are of great interest in providing indications as to whether one should invest in actively managed or index funds. They also can be expected to provide critical evidence on the desirability of investing via an individual stock portfolio in general. If the actively managed funds run by professionals can't beat the averages, how much chance does a typical investment advisor, or the average investor, have?

While there are a great many studies evaluating the performance of actively managed funds, they all tend to reach similar conclusions. A classic study by Michael C. Jensen[1] in 1967 studied the performance of 115 mutual funds from 1945 to 1964, comparing their performance to stock market averages. In his studies, he developed and used a numeric termed *Jensen's Alpha*, which is a measure of the risk-adjusted excess rate of return of a mutual fund compared to averages. The bottom line was as follows:

"*The evidence on mutual fund performance indicates not only that these 115 mutual funds were on average not able to predict security prices well enough to outperform a buy-the-market-and-hold policy, but also that there is very little evidence that any individual fund was able to do significantly better than that which we expected from mere random chance.*"[2]

A larger study reported in 1996[3] on a larger number (279) of mutual funds. The study was largely concerned with the problem of why individuals continue to invest in actively managed funds, since they do not outperform market indices. Major conclusions, however, included confirmation that actively managed mutual funds offer, on the average, a negative rate of return relative to market indices, and that index funds give the investor a better deal.

2. Burton Malkiel, in his investing classic *A Random Walk Down Wall Street*[4], presents a great deal of data supporting the futility of active portfolio management and the superior performance of index stock mutual funds. Included in the compelling data he presents is a detailed comparison of actively managed stock fund performance versus a very broadly based U.S. market index, the Wilshire 5000, from 1973 to 1994. Over this period, about two-thirds of the actively managed funds underperformed the market index (Figure 4-2).

   Malkiel even reports a number of studies in which pure chance selection of securities prospectively beat the market averages, including one by the editors of *Forbes* magazine in 1967, in which darts were thrown at the stock-market page.

3. Other compilations of the performance of actively managed funds compared to the S&P 500 Index are available in contemporary books on stock investing. John Bogle, the American father of index fund investing, has summarized the performance of actively managed U.S. stock mutual funds from 1963 to 1998[5], in a manner similar to that of Malkiel above. In most years (21 out of 35), actively managed funds failed to perform as well as the S&P 500 Index.

4. There have been efforts to improve performance with actively managed funds by investing in those that have outperformed the market recently. This concept, which has been called "chasing

performance," has been shown not to work well over the longer term. There tends to be a reversion to the mean over time, with the funds with recent superior performance simply unable to keep it up[6].

An interesting ongoing study that provides an indication of the ineffectiveness of chasing performance is a study by Dimensional Fund Advisors and S&P/Micropay, which evaluated the subsequent performance of the top-performing mutual funds over the previous five years, and evaluates their subsequent performance over the next five years compared to the S&P 500 Average,

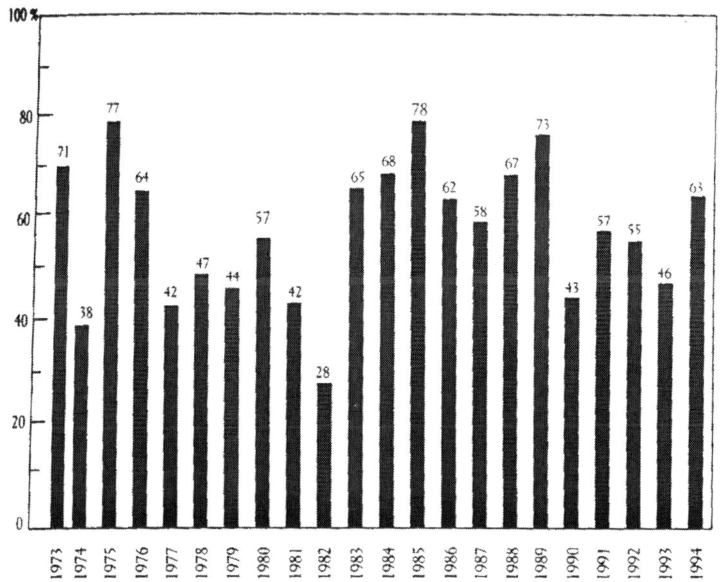

Figure 4-2: The percentage of actively managed mutual funds beaten by the broadly based Wilshire 5000 index, 1973 to 1994.

Source: Malkiel, B. 1996. *A Random Walk Down Wall Street.* New York: W.W. Norton. Page 215.

and to all funds[7]. The purpose here was to determine whether past performance over the last five years could be used to predict future performance. When this analysis was performed over five-year periods from 1975 to 1995, no advantage of investing in the 30 past performers was noted; in each period tested, the subsequent performance of the 30 prior top performers did not keep up with the S&P 500 Average (Figure 4-3). Clearly, "past performance is no guarantee of future results." In this case, the traditional disclaimer attached to most investment advertisements is all too true.

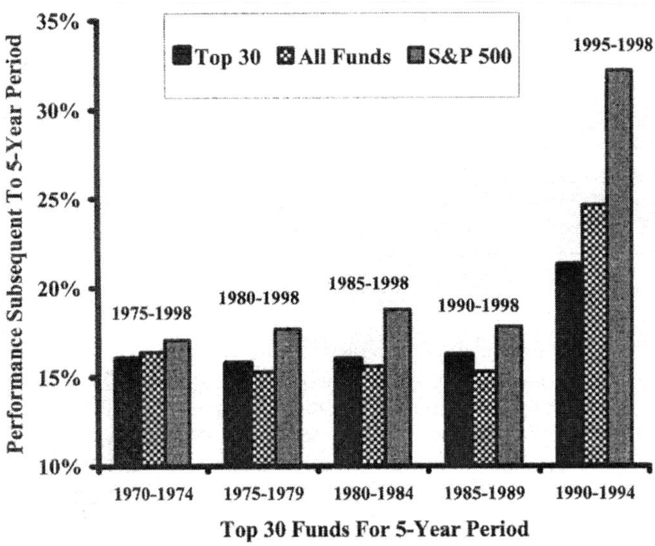

Figure 4-3: Subsequent performance over five years for the 30 funds that had the best performance over the previous five years in the U.S. market, compared to all funds and the S&P 500 Average. The clear implication is that there is no significant value to investing in funds based on their past performance.

Source: Bernstein, W. 2002. *The Four Pillars of Investing.* New York: McGraw-Hill. Page 81.

5. William Bernstein has also summarized the performance of the nation's pension funds, using data provided by Piscataqua Research[8]. These funds represent an enormous pool, larger than the aggregate of all the nation's mutual funds, and managed by top managers. In this comparison, the 60/40 mix of stocks and bonds characterizing 243 large pension funds in the United States was compared to a standard benchmark of 60% S&P 500 and 40% Lehman Bond Index. The results, shown graphically below (Figure 4-4), indicate that more than 90% of these funds underperformed the benchmark S&P 500 Average.

The above data provides solid evidence that professional investors don't seem to be able to outperform the market via a stock selection approach.

Can't We Just Follow the Advice of Analysts or Do Our Own Research?

Let's consider the products created by today's professional stock market analysts; they seem to suffer from the equivalent of grade inflation in our schools and universities. In a recent article in the *New York Times* concerning analysts' recommendations, Randy Cass of First Coverage says,

"It doesn't matter if you're in a bear market, a bull market, or a flat market, you're going to get 95% of the research coming out telling you to buy, it's just the way it's always been."[9]

The article goes on to note that this unfortunate tendency to overrate stocks has always existed, and that analysts were strongly recommending

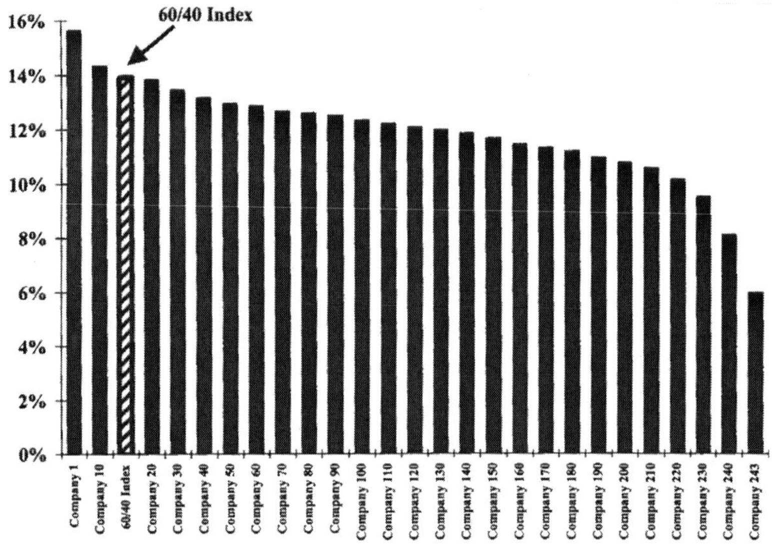

Figure 4-4: Performance of a representative number of a total of 243 large pension funds in the United States compared to a standard benchmark (the 60/40 Index) that represents the results which would be achieved by merely investing in market averages, not pursuing any active selective selection of stocks and bonds at all. The remarkable fact is that the large majority of the managed pension funds underperform the average rate of return.

Source: Bernstein, W. 2002. *The Four Pillars of Investing*, p.86. New York: McGraw-Hill.

stocks that would experience severe drops just before the tech stock bust in 2000. They also missed completely the severe market drop in 2008, as you can see in Figure 4-5, in which their sell recommendations hovered just under 6% during and before this entire period.

An important reason for the inflated ratings on stocks is the conflict of interest for many analysts resulting from the fact that their companies may be involved in businesses that generate large fees from the very companies they are supposed to be assessing. From the wonderful book (later adapted into a movie) *The Smartest Guys in the Room*, concerning the evaluation of Enron stock, comes this quote: "Over time, many companies came to expect "buy" recommendations from analysts; it was often a prerequisite for getting banking business."[10]

This sort of conflict of interest for analysts—between the need for objective evaluation of companies and the profitable business collaborations of many of the analysts' firms—has long been recognized as one of the root causes of the lack of analysts' objectivity. Although efforts have been made to reduce this conflict of interest, it likely is still an important factor.

If one then concludes that the best approach is to bypass the analysts and go directly to interpretation of company data, one will only have to recall again the Enron example, in which the data was not only impenetrable, but ultimately shown to be fraudulent. Unfortunately, there are many other examples of such misrepresentation.

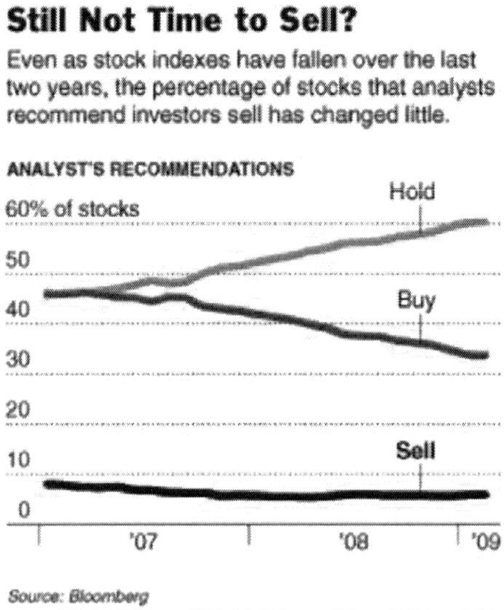

Figure 4-5: Percentages of stock analysts recommending hold, buy, or sell recommendations over the past two years. Sell recommendations are consistently at only about a 6% level. There has and been little change in the overall assessment by analysts before and during a time of severe drops in market prices.

Source: Healy J, Grynbaum MM, Why analysts keep telling investors to buy. *The New York Times*, February 9, 2009.

Is There Really No Analytic Service with a Winning Record of Stock Recommendations, and How Can We Know for Sure?

Although it is hard to believe that the long-term comprehensive overvaluation of the prospects of individual stocks, as shown above for stock analysts, can be useful in selecting stocks, it is hard to prove that analysts' recommendations are not at all useful. To do this, one would have to follow a large number of stocks recommended by analysts over time to see how the recommendations have worked out.

It is possible to perform such an evaluation in selected cases, however. Value Line is a respected American company that has provided concise summaries of many U.S. stocks on a continuing basis for many years. A great many individuals, including Warren Buffet[11], find these succinct summaries of companies very useful in their personal investing. One feature of the Value Line analysis provides insight into the potential of fundamental analysis to provide incremental returns on stocks over time. The Value Line analysis includes an estimation of stock "timeliness," rated from 1 (best) to 5 (worst). This timeliness rating represents a very well-organized and orderly evaluation over time of the relative desirability of purchase of a wide range of stocks. Can we tell how well this system of stock selection has worked in practice?

It turns out that we can check on how well the timeliness rating works over time because Value Line also runs several mutual funds. One of these is the Value Line Fund, which uses a strategy based on the timeliness rating. Only stocks with the most favorable timeliness rating are purchased and maintained in this fund. On the website advertising the Value Line Fund, there is the implication that the timeliness system may lead to substantially improved returns over the S&P 500 Average over the years. The most recent annual report for the Value Line Fund, however, indicates that the rate of return for this fund over the last ten years has, in fact, underperformed the S&P 500 Average by 1.8% per annum.

Is Even More Evidence Required?

There is in fact a great deal of further data that confirms the clear implications of the above information, but perhaps I have presented enough at this point to convince. It should be clear that active management of a stock portfolio by stock selection is not a winning strategy. You can be certain that the highly trained and capable professionals who actively manage mutual funds and the large U.S. pension funds have the most expertise, and the best access to high-quality company data, available anywhere. If these professionals cannot beat the market averages, what are the chances that you as an individual investor, or your financial advisor, will be any more successful over the long term? We would be fooling ourselves if we thought either route would likely be more successful than simply buying index funds such as S&P 500 Index funds, which mirror the broad market.

If you need even further attestation to the futility of stock selection as a tool to enhance investment returns, you might consider testimonials from some of the most accomplished and respected stock analysts and stock pickers in modern history. Benjamin Graham is the author of the classic text *The Intelligent Investor*, described as "the best book ever written on stock market investing" by Warren Buffet. Mr. Graham was in fact Mr. Buffet's mentor, and the modern father of stock and stock market analysis. Near the end of his life, he wrote,

"I am no longer an advocate of elaborate techniques of security analysis in order to find superior value opportunities . . . I doubt whether such extensive efforts will generate sufficiently superior selections to justify their cost . . . I'm on the side of the "efficient market" school of thought."[12]

THE EFFICIENT MARKET SCHOOL OF THOUGHT

The efficient market school of thought concerning stock market valuation is really quite a simple principle. The basic concept is that all currently available information concerning an individual stock is widely known, and the implications of this information are already reflected in a stock's price.

While the principle is simple, and is likely to be generally true, there are rather profound implications for individual investors. Any attempt by an individual or a fund manager to gain an edge in stock selection is likely to be futile, since all the information on which a purchase/sale decision might be made is generally available, and the only possibility of superior investment performance can be superior analytic techniques applied to the available data.

As we have seen from the data presented, consistently superior performance in stock selection seems a distinct rarity, implying that superior analytic techniques capable of consistently enhancing returns from stock investing are little in evidence.

There is no more honored stock picker than Peter Lynch, who was the celebrated manager of the huge and hugely successful Fidelity Magellan fund for many years. After retirement from managing Fidelity Magellan, Lynch admitted that most investors would be better off in an index fund than an actively managed fund.[13]

It Is Easy to Fool Ourselves About Our Investment Performance

While the data and opinions summarized above provide compelling evidence of the poor chances of outperforming the markets via stock selection, we are still likely to meet individual investors or advisors who claim that they are able to perform this feat. In the days when I tried to outperform using stock selection, I found that I would often be basically fooling myself when I looked at my overall market performance from selected stocks. It is not hard to do this after you have sold off most of your dogs, conveniently forgotten about them, and just look at the relative winners you have left.

When I hear this general claim now, I am reminded of the stories I often hear from folks returning from a Las Vegas junket. Very seldom does anyone claim to have lost money; reports are generally of a winning streak. We all know, though, that the gaudy surroundings in the casinos of Vegas were not financed by a losing strategy. Similarly, it is all too easy to use psychological defense mechanisms to avoid the truth of having lost money in investments. It may not be possible to check on the veracity of an individual or an advisor, but when we are able to evaluate credible data, the only viable conclusion is that stock selection simply does not work as a strategy for enhancing rate of return.

Two Other Important Factors Favoring Stock Index Mutual Funds

It gets even worse for actively managed funds and custodial accounts run by financial advisors/brokers when one takes account of their various fees. These will be discussed more fully in Chapter 5, but consider for now that index funds tracking the S&P 500 Average, for example, are available with management expense ratios (MERs) under .2% per year, whereas the average actively managed U.S. stock fund charges 1.2 to 1.3%—six times as much. The expenses charged for custodial accounts are in the range of the active funds or higher.

Yet another factor clearly favoring stock index mutual funds is tax efficiency compared to actively managed funds. While turnover of stocks is rare in stock index funds, since these are quite stable in composition, because they track a rarely varying index of stocks, actively managed funds have annual turnover ratios of about 85%. This high turnover ratio guarantees long- and short-term capital gains that will flow through to the investor and result in harmful tax consequences compared to those for the holder of a comparable stock index fund[14].

It should be pretty clear that the only sensible choice for the stock market portion of our investing is in low-fee stock index mutual funds.

Bonds and Bond Funds

Debt instruments issued by governments and corporations are the vehicles for the fixed-income portion of our portfolio, with a small allocation to a money market fund. Compared to stocks, bonds are in many ways rather straightforward. They are classified mainly according to yield, quality, and duration. In the bond world, the principle that the rate of return is proportional to the degree of risk is very clear. The yields of high-yield-high-risk (junk) bonds exceed those of intermediate-risk/yield investment–grade corporate bonds, which in turn exceed the yields and risk of highest-quality government bonds.

Some advocate buying individual bonds directly, since one may obtain higher yields when avoiding management costs, but the simpler approach is to invest via a bond fund or bond index fund[15]. A bond fund will consist of a large number of bonds of a particular type (government, corporate, etc.) and defined quality (from rating agencies; AAA is the highest), with bond durations extending over a particular range of time (short is one to two years, intermediate is two to ten years, and long is more than ten years).

A bond fund allows you to readily purchase—or switch from stocks into—a desired bond portfolio, and the characteristics of the bonds in that portfolio will be maintained over time. If you purchase, for example, a fund of short-term investment-grade corporate bonds, the characteristics of the fund will be maintained over the years by the fund company in terms of the bond duration and other characteristics. If you purchased individual bonds, their individual durations will decrease over time. They will come due, and you will have to purchase more bonds. If you trade between stock index funds and bond funds of the same U.S. mutual fund, there will generally not be any trading fees. If you are trying to make this a simple as possible, the fund approach is better because it is simpler.

There are two further key points in bond fund investing, apart from the risk/yield trade-off. It is best to purchase bond funds that are relatively short term and that have very low fees. It is true that long-term bonds pay a premium in interest over shorter-term bonds, since investors demand a reward for taking on the risk of the longer ownership. The risk of longer ownership with longer-term bonds, however, is that interest rates might rise in the future and the price of the long-term bonds will then go down significantly.

In bond fund ownership, you should seek a sweet spot balancing yield and interest rate risk, which is the possibility of decline in bonds associated with rising rates. The relative advantage in yield is usually greatest for a duration of about five years[16]; you will get reasonable yields with reasonable interest rate risk with a duration of about five years or less. Duration of a bond is a key parameter; it expresses the sensitivity of the bond to changes in interest rates. This parameter differs from bond maturity, and is determined by a relatively complex process to indicate the change in value that will result from a 1% change in interest rates. For example, a five-year duration means that a 1% increase in interest rates will cause a 5% decrease in the bond price. Since interest rates are so unpredictable, risk is limited by limiting duration.

It seems reasonable to compromise on bond quality/safety as well as duration in order to obtain reasonable risk and reward. Bond funds consisting of short to intermediate investment-grade corporate bonds seem a good compromise, both in terms of bond durations and bond quality. To keep some portion of the bond money even safer, short-term federal bonds will work, and a smaller portion in short to intermediate high-yield bonds can provide more return at higher risk.

The second key rule of bond fund investing, keeping fees very low, may not always be easy to achieve, but it is especially critical to keep costs low in bond funds. The main reason is that bonds pay relatively low rates of return, so you just can't afford large fees. There is little that management skill can accomplish in increasing the rate of return of a bond fund, so you shouldn't be paying for such presumed skills. You need to check the details of a fund before purchase to make sure the fees are acceptable. Criteria for acceptability include no back- or front-load fees, no 12b-1 fees (used for advertising), and an MER (management expense ratio) of .5 or less. Unfortunately, too few bond funds meet these criteria. If you have the ability to exploit them, the bond funds of Vanguard have low-fee structures.

Other types of bond funds may be considered; bond index funds are similar to stock index funds in that they simply attempt to track a bond market index such as the Barclays U.S. Aggregate Bond Index, tracked by Vanguard Total Bond Market Index Fund, which currently has an MER of .19%. There are very few such funds, but these tend to represent very good value, since they typically have very low fees and will generally closely track their target index, providing good returns.

Municipal bond funds are free of national tax, or free of both state and national taxes. They are worthwhile for the higher marginal rate investors in taxable accounts.

CHAPTER 5

THE FOUR DEADLY HORSEMEN OF INVESTING

It has been said that the four deadly horsemen of investing are taxes, inflation, fees, and risk. The meaning is that these factors are all potential hazards to successful investing. The nature of the dangers they represent can only be mitigated if we have some understanding of how each of these horsemen can be harmful to us. It is difficult, in fact, to develop an effective investment system without consideration of the four horsemen.

Horseman #1: Taxes

We can likely imagine a rational tax system for the United States. It might include two or three progressive tax brackets, a standard deduction large enough to allow the relatively poor to avoid taxation, no other deductions allowable at all, and consideration of all income streams equally, on the premise that a buck is a buck. What we have in reality, and what we have to deal with, is not a tax system that can be summarized in one sentence, but one that requires many thousands of pages and is virtually incomprehensible to all but the highly trained. It is unfortunately unavoidable that we at least must know the basics of the effects of this system of taxation on our investments.

The system I will ultimately be proposing is one based on stock index funds and bond funds. The types of taxation relevant to such funds include taxes on the proceeds from the sale of funds that have appreciated

THE FORTUNATE FEW

There are only seven states with no income tax at all: Alaska, Florida, Nevada, South Dakota, Texas, Washington, and Wyoming.

The tax structures of the remaining states, including the rates, income streams to which state taxation is applied, and allowable deductions, are highly variable among the individual states. California (where I live) has a top marginal state tax rate of 9.3%—among the highest in the nation.

The state portion of income taxation can represent a substantial burden on investment income, since as noted above, there is generally no lower rate applied to long-term capital gains. In New Hampshire and Tennessee, the state income tax is limited to dividend and interest income, but not to other revenue sources such as salaries[1].

or depreciated in value, as well as taxes on stock dividends and bond interest. Federal and state governments tax sources of revenue from both stocks and bonds separately, and taxation by the federal government and individual states differs.

At the federal level, capital gains or losses on stocks or bonds held less than one year are considered short-term, and are taxed as regular income with a current top marginal rate (percent taxation on the last [most recent] dollar of income) of 35%. If the security is held for a year or more, the capital gain is considered long-term, and the maximum tax rate is 15%; at the federal level, stock dividends are taxed at a maximum rate of 15%. Bond interest, on the other hand, is generally taxed as regular income.

Taxes at the state level are at lower levels than the federal government, but do not generally allow for lower rates of taxation for stock dividends and long-term capital gains compared to regular income. All revenue from investment is generally taxed at the regular rate by the states.

How Taxation Affects Mutual Fund Returns

Since we are considering investment in stock and bond funds, it is important to understand how capital gains/losses, dividends on stock, and interest on bonds in such funds generate taxes at the state and federal levels. In a stock or bond fund, trading in individual securities occurs throughout the year, generating both long- and short-term capital gains and losses. Additionally, of course, stock dividends and bond interest are paid throughout the year. Each year, your share of the capital gains, dividends, and interest generated by a particular fund is reported to the government, and you are responsible for taxation of your share of these revenues flowing through to you. The taxation is, of course, at both the state and federal levels, and the amount of taxation is a function of the amounts of revenues, their classification (e.g., long-term capital gain, interest), and the level of taxation at the state and federal levels.

Some funds generate considerably more taxation than others, largely on the basis of stock turnover during the year. Funds that have a high turnover rate (percentage change in portfolio composition) over the year generate more capital gains and losses of the long- and short-term varieties. High turnover generates not only substantial transaction costs, but also high tax rates for the fund holders, since the capital gains ultimately flow through to them.

It is noteworthy that actively managed stock funds in the United States have relatively high turnover rates of about 85% per year, whereas stock index funds have much lower turnover rates. The reason that index funds have lower turnover rates is that these funds need to trade little to attain a mix of stock that closely tracks a desired index, whereas actively managed funds tend to trade frequently in (generally futile) efforts to maximize fund performance.

The tax advantages of stock index mutual funds compared to actively managed funds are substantial, and are another important reason to favor such funds, beyond the superior long-term performance they give, and the very low fees many of them charge. As discussed in Chapter 4, the rates of return of actively managed funds tend to underperform the general market, so we are not benefitting very much, if at all, from the high turnover rates of these funds.

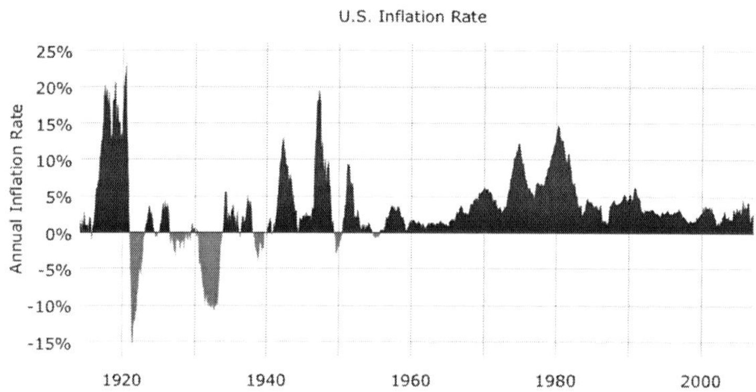

Figure 5-1: Inflation/deflation rates in the United States from 1910 to the present day. The rates have been highly variable, with significant deflationary periods from 1920 to 1940.

Source: http://en.wikipedia.org/wiki/File:U.S._Historical_Inflation.svg

Horseman #2: Inflation (or Deflation)

U.S. inflation, the annual change in price levels as measured by the consumer price index (CPI), is plotted above (figure 5-1) from 1912 to present day.

As shown, inflation has been quite variable over the years in the United States, and there have been significant periods of deflation, or decreasing price levels, accompanying and following the depression of the 1930s.

In recent years, inflation has averaged about 3%. There has been some concern recently that there may be danger of deflation in the United States, since general price levels have seen significant declines in the past year[2]. Deflation, if it occurs, would be a very serious problem, since it is difficult for government to fight it. In general deflation, both real and financial assets tend to stagnate or decline in value; individuals feel relatively poorer and averse to the kind of risk-taking that could be stimulatory. Deflation and near-deflation has been a serious issue in Japan ever since the bursting of the real estate and stock bubbles around 1990, and it has proved quite intractable. Government has attempted to provide the stimulus needed for expansion, largely through capital projects whose cost has expanded federal debt to almost 200% of GDP (gross domestic product), an extremely high level.

Both deflation and a significant increase in inflation would have very serious consequences for our investment strategy, since markets historically do poorly during either condition. U.S. stock markets, for example, performed poorly in the 1970s when inflation was very high, and the Japanese market has decreased at present to about one-quarter of the 1990 value during Japan's long struggle with deflation.

Unfortunately, inflation (or deflation) is one of those dominant economic factors that appears very difficult to predict by economists or other seers. The record of prediction is quite poor regarding inflation, currency fluctuations, and the general course of the overall U.S. and world economies. Since we can have little idea of what to expect, we can only take a few precautionary measures. One important step is the limitation of our bond maturities to about five years, since a recurrence of inflation will likely be accompanied by a rise in interest rates and declines in longer-term bond prices.

Only "Real" Rates of Return Really Matter Over Time

It is important to recognize and account for inflation over the years; the only returns that have meaning to us are the "real," or inflation-corrected, values of returns, since the correction for inflation controls for changes over time in purchasing power. As will be discussed more fully later in this chapter, this is one of the critical correction factors that must be applied to a stated or "nominal" rate of return in order to determine a more realistic value. If the cost of living goes up 3% per year, we must account for this annual decrease in purchasing power, and correct the stated rate of return downward by 3% to account for its effects. Otherwise, we will be in danger of fooling ourselves into thinking our investing results are better than they really are.

Figure 5-2: The dramatic effects of inflation on real rates of return from stocks are illustrated in plots of the inflation-adjusted and nominal DJIA over 100 years. While the nominal DJIA has gone up more than 100-fold, the real increase has only been about 5-fold.

Source: Reddy, S. Amid Pressing Problems, Threat of Deflation Looms. *Wall Street Journal.* October 18, 2008.

As pointed out in a recent article in the *Wall Street Journal*[3], the Dow Jones Industrial Average is currently at a similar level to that of 1999. When one accounts for the effects of inflation over the 10-year period, however, the Dow is only now at an inflation-adjusted level of 8200, and would have to rise another 28% or so to get back to the levels of 1999. Similarly, the nominal returns of stocks over longer periods appear (misleadingly) much higher than the real inflation-adjusted rates. One might think that the low real rates achievable with stock investing should make us avoid the stock market entirely, but if we evaluate the alternative investments of municipal, corporate, and government bonds, we will find their real rates of return even lower than stocks. An idea of the dramatically lower real, compared to nominal, stock market returns can be seen in Figure 5-2, from the article referenced[4].

Horseman #3: Risk

When I've talked to people about risk in investing, many express the opinion that they are not interested in any risky investments; they're interested in investing sensibly and conservatively, definitely not in gambling.

Investing or Gambling?

We might ask just what gambling is, and how different is it from investing. There are many similar definitions of gambling. Here are two from the Merriam Webster's online dictionary:

Gamble: Take a risk in the hope of a favorable outcome. Play for stakes in the hope of winning.

So, the basic element is the taking of risk in return for the chance of profit. As you will see, this element is always present in investment.

In fact, a bedrock principle of investing is that there is a strong correlation between risk and reward; one has to incur incremental risk to obtain incremental reward.

A definition of risk seems in order, since I've seen it used in ways different from the expected when applied to investment. Sometimes risk in investing is interpreted as asset volatility, or the degree of change in value over time, but that is not what we are generally thinking of when we buy a stock or bond. We generally mean something like the likelihood that we will suffer an effective loss of all or part of the real capital value of our investment. When I refer to "risk" without a modifier, that is what I will mean. There are various subcategories of risk, such as interest rate risk, in which rising rates cause the value of bond assets to decline, and currency risk of an asset denominated in U.S. currency, which might fall in value relative to currencies of other countries.

Risk in return for profit becomes unavoidable as soon as you have saved some money and put it into some kind of investment vehicle, or even if you have put it under your mattress. While virtually all investors are more or less aware that risk is present in investment, there may not be general appreciation of the fact that risk must be incurred in investing in order to gain rewards; there is no escape.

When you look closely at the issue of risk, you will see that risk is not necessarily a bad thing; it is in reality a critical factor to take into consideration and to be managed wisely by the successful investor.

Risk in Investing: Cautionary Tales

I've learned a bit about risk from my personal experience as well as reading. My grandfather was a great businessman, but he had a penchant for buying on a whim substantial amounts of stock in companies that were the longest of long shots. Recently, on going through a safety deposit box after a death in the family, I came across certificates for substantial numbers of shares of such success stories (not) as "Canadian Kodiak Petroleum" and "Carmel West Petroleum." My lawyer friend, who found these with me, said that a great many families have such useless stock certificates that they have found in deposit boxes; some people paper a wall with them.

This is a classic example of the sort of risky investment that is widely acknowledged: an extremely high-risk investment going for the big score, but ultimately leading to a loss of all invested capital. The degree of risk here was so high as to seem a bit ridiculous in retrospect, although the rewards might have been commensurate if any of these fliers had worked out.

A recent article in the *Wall Street Journal* illustrates the opposite problem: what happens when we practice extreme risk aversion. This article, entitled "When 401(k) Investing Goes Bad," described the experience of school workers in West Virginia who had been offered a new pension plan of the 401(k) type to replace their traditional fixed government pensions 17 years ago[5]. The workers apparently felt quite uncertain about appropriate investment choices, but an overriding concern was the avoidance of any loss of capital. Substantial funds were put into annuities, which are a very conservative low-yield investment, typically with high fees. Other vehicles were used as well, for which the invested capital was completely safe, but yields were low, with no real prospect of appreciation. Over the 17-year period, of course, the stock market experienced some big increases in which this group did not participate.

At the end of 2007, the median balance was only $34,420 for workers over the age of 60—sums that would have resulted in very small payouts to this group. Almost incredibly, and very fortunately for the group of school workers, the legislature of the state passed a resolution that allowed the workers to switch back to the old-style government plan with its much higher monthly payouts after retirement.

In a *Frontline* program on 401(k) investing by Hedrick Smith, a similar experience in Nebraska was reported, in which a standard defined-benefit (DB) pension and a 401(k) plan were run concurrently[6]. The 401(k) plan again suffered from the inexperience and risk aversion of the participants. At the end of the experiment, the 401(k) option was deemed a failure, and this option was terminated for state workers.

Risk Is a Requirement for Success

The lesson here is that some diversification into higher-risk/higher-reward investments is required over the longer term, or rates of return will be poor. If the workers in either Virginia or Nebraska had chosen a significant stock market exposure, they would have participated in substantial stock market runups during the plan periods.

In the investing plan described in this book, the vehicles available to us will be index stock funds and bond funds. Sound investment clearly involves managing in an intelligent manner the trade-off between risk and reward. Stocks are riskier, but offer more reward potential in the long term, as noted in Chapter 4, and these will be emphasized in the investing system.

The system will do its best to take advantage of the potential rewards of stocks while using diversification and market timing to mitigate risk.

Horseman #4: Fees

There has long been the impression that money managers of various types benefit from their dealings to a much greater extent than their clients. This perception was noted in the popular book *Where Are the Customers' Yachts?* published by Fred Schwed Jr. in 1940[7].

"Once in the dear dead days beyond recall, an out-of-town visitor was being shown the wonders of the New York financial district. When the party arrived at the Battery, one of his guides indicated some handsome ships riding at anchor. He said, 'Look, those are the bankers' and brokers' yachts.' 'Where are the customers' yachts?' asked the naïve visitor."

The Fees We Pay Have a Critical Impact on Our Overall Rates of Return

The effects of the various fees on investments over time are likely under-appreciated; they can be among the deadliest of the four horsemen. In our financial dealings, we may pay transactions costs to stockbrokers (discount or otherwise) or mutual funds. We may pay management fees to mutual funds, and we may hire the services of financial advisors, planners, or "wealth managers" who may also take on the shared responsibility for our investments and manage our portfolios. Although there are many names for the individuals whom we pay to help us invest, I will refer to all as "advisors" in this chapter.

In the investment strategy outlined in this book, we are planning to trade among several of the stock index funds of one or more very low-fee mutual fund companies. In this environment, one should also consider fund purchase and redemption fees. Although the types of funds I will be discussing do not generally have purchase fees, there are a few with limitations on trading out of the fund sooner than within a defined period, and we must check for these.

Harnessing This Horseman: Keeping Fees Low As Possible

When dealing with a large fund group such as Vanguard or Fidelity (the two largest firms in the United States) and using the techniques I advocate—which involve switching occasionally between different funds in the same fund group—many of the above fees are absent or minimal and can almost be disregarded. I will use Vanguard and Fidelity funds in the examples I will provide in this book. There are many other equally attractive low-fee funds you may want to investigate in your planning.

None of the index funds I will suggest charge 12b-1 fees, and transaction fees for switching from one fund to another are either absent or minimal. You will do a little better at these firms if you have substantial capital, not unexpectedly. At the present time, if you have at least $100,000 invested in a single fund (say, the 500 Index Fund), you qualify for a lower annual MER. The annual MER for the Vanguard S&P 500 Index Fund is currently .15%, but only .07% if you have more than $100,000 in the fund. Fidelity has a Spartan 500 Index Fund that has only a .10% MER, and a $10,000 minimum.

If these management rates seem very competitive and low, they certainly are. In the bad old days, as described in Chapter 2, there were very high front-end and/or back-end load fees of at least several percent (basically a poorly hidden transaction cost), and a high annual MER of 2% or more. As noted in Chapter 4, these very high fees have never been associated with increased rates of return over the years, and one might wonder what we thought we were paying for back in the high-fee era, which is still receding from view but not gone.

FEES CHARGED BY MUTUAL FUNDS

As you will be seeing, the fee beast should not be underestimated in its voracious tendency to eat into our rates of return. In order to take the measure of the beast, a summary of the various component fees affecting our mutual fund investments is in order.

Load fees: These are fees charged by the fund company, as a percentage of capital invested, when one either purchases or sells one of their mutual funds. If charged when buying, it is called a front-end load, and if when selling, it is called a back-end load.

12(b)-1 fees: These are special fees charged by mutual funds to pay for fund advertising.

Transaction costs: If one sends their money to a typical fund company such as Vanguard or Fidelity, there will be no transaction costs typically charged for initial purchase of a fund or exchanges from one fund to another. There will be transaction costs for trading an ETF

Since the transaction fees for occasional fund switching are absent or small, and load fees can be avoided, the remaining key fee for us to consider is the annual MER. From the above discussion of the MERs of the S&P 500 Index funds, we might assume that in the present day, fees on all funds are very low . . . and we would be wrong. The average MER for large actively managed funds consisting of a broad range of U.S. stocks is about 1.2%—at least a full percentage point more than for low fee index funds.

(exchange-traded fund), since these entities are bought and sold in a similar manner to individual stocks. Such transactions costs can be minimized by using a discount broker.

Short-term trading fees: These are fees, expressed as a percentage of capital, that are charged when one sells a fund within a stated time period after purchase. For example, a fund may charge a 1% fee if one trades out of a specific fund within 90 days of purchase.

Management fees: These are usually the most important type of fee for the situations we will be considering: investing in stock index mutual funds. The fee, expressed as a percentage of capital, is charged each year by management. In many stock index funds, there are various classes of shares, with the lowest fees assessed for the classes requiring more capital invested. The management fee, or management expense ratio (MER), can be as low as less than .1% and as high as 1 to 2% (and even higher) for many actively managed mutual funds.

Calculation of a Meaningful Likely Future Rate of Return and the Effects of High Fees

The "wealth management" industry, which includes a wide range of firms, seems currently to be an expanding enterprise, at a time when few others are. It is hard to pay attention to the media for any length of time without exposure to the numerous ads for financial services companies. It is no mystery why such ads and such companies are so plentiful; it is a very

THE HIGH FEE CHAMPS OF THE MUTUAL FUND INDUSTRY

If we want to find the real high-fee champions for fund fees, we may have to go up to my native Canada, where the average expense ratio for such funds is over 2%. According to a 2008 article, "Mutual Fund Fees Around the World," the average expense ratio for Canadian Funds is a whopping 2.56%[8]. Some Canadian funds have recently cut these fees a bit, but the largest fund in Canada for example, Investor's Dividend Fund, still has a MER of 2.71%.

Previously, in Chapter 4, we noted that it is even more important that bond funds have low fees, compared to stock funds. The reason is that the overall rate of the return is generally lower for bonds, and we really can't afford high fees. What are the levels of Canadian bond fund fees? Note is made of this by a Canadian financial expert, in a recent article[9] in the Toronto Globe and Mail:

"He notes that a five-year Government of Canada bond has a yield of 2.5 per cent for much of the year, while the average cost of owning a Canadian bond mutual fund is 1.7 per cent. 'You're taking 70 per cent of the returns, and that won't work.'"

It is hard to imagine the reasons behind the continuance of such high management fees; we know they are most unlikely to be justified by superior fund performance, since such funds rarely outperform the market, as detailed in Chapter 4. It is probably that investors in such funds simply do not appreciate the very high levels of the fees they are paying, and the very serious impact of such fees on their rates of return. Those investing in such funds will be providing substantial contributions toward yacht purchases by fund management, but will very likely receive mediocre returns for themselves.

If a Canadian mutual fund investor is wondering where to invest his or her money, the best thing to do may be to buy an exchange-traded fund (ETF) through a discount broker (to minimize transaction costs) that tracks an index such as the Toronto Stock Index or the American S&P 500 Average.

An ETF is a type of mutual fund traded on exchanges like stocks, and many of them track stock market indices such as those in which we are interested. The value of the funds tends closely to follow the value of the underlying assets—the stocks in the fund portfolio. Although these funds are increasingly popular, their overall capitalization is a small fraction of conventional mutual funds'.

ETFs offer Canadian investors the possibility of escaping from the sky-high fees charged by regular Canadian mutual funds. You can find a listing of Canadian ETFs at the following URL: http://etf.stock-encyclopedia.com/category/etfs-listed-in-canada.html.

lucrative business. We've documented in Chapter 4 that active portfolio management generally provides performance inferior to the overall market, in which we can invest via low-fee index funds. Here we'll examine just how much this ineffectual management costs us, and it's a lot.

To understand why this is so, let's look at the numbers relevant to a managed investment account today. It is important to figure out the factors involved in determining the rate of return we are receiving, and to understand how much of the returns are really going to ourselves—the

Figure 5-3: While in the long term, stocks have historically outperformed bonds, there has been a recent convergence of rates of return to around 5% in real (inflation-adjusted) terms.

Source: Fairfield, H. "For a Retirement Plan, Stocks = Top Returns (Usually)." *New York Times*. October 19, 2008.

investors—and how much are going to advisors. Then we'll have to ask just what we are getting for the fees we are paying to advisors.

Figure 5-3 from the *New York Times*[10] was created with data from Gary Burtless at the Brookings Institution and the National Bureau of Economic Research. The chart plots the rates of return of stocks, bonds, and a 50/50 mix of the two instruments over a 100-year period.

Each point on the chart above indicates the real (inflation-adjusted) annual rate of return of these investment choices. While the chart indicates the general superiority of stock investing over the 100 years plotted, we should note that at the present time, the rate of return on all three options is converging to a real value of about 5%, due to relatively poor stock market performance over the past ten years. While there are many things we can learn from this chart, right now we'll use it only to indicate a likely real rate of stock and bond return in the future (5% per annum), perhaps ten years or so.

Your Actual Rate of Return Is Probably Not What You Think

Unless we think that times are going to change, and perhaps get much better very soon, it would seem reasonable to predict a conservative real rate of return on stock and bond investment approximating 5% in the future. If we assume that the long-term average pattern of inflation will persist in the future, we must take this into account. The long-term average of about 3% inflation, then, will require that our investments are far enough along the risk/reward continuum to generate an 8% nominal (preinflation) return. As we account for the various factors diminishing our rates of return (the Deadly Horsemen), the calculated rates become progressively more realistic, but progressively smaller as well.

Since it seems clear that a realistic rate of return can only be calculated by subtracting the harmful effects of taxes, inflation, and fees, we must do our best to allow for the decrements due to these three variables. Let us consider a taxable account for the purposes of our calculations, with the stated real average rate of return of 5%, the mean value in recent years as discussed above. If we assume inflation of 3% per year, we will have a nominal rate of 8%. We will first consider the effects of taxes, which of course are paid on the nominal rate of return.

What will be the effect of taxation on the 8% nominal return? The actual taxes paid per year are a function of the mix of long- and short-term capital gains in the portfolio—with the long-term gains generally receiving more favorable treatment, as well as the mix of classes of regular income (dividends, interest). Total taxes will also depend on the level of state taxation, which does not generally provide more favorable tax treatment for long-term gains, or for stock dividends.

The marginal rates (rates on the last dollar earned), which are the relevant rates for individuals, will differ for individuals that have different incomes, of course. An overall rate of 25% seems a reasonable estimate for the average investor, based on current federal and state tax rates, perhaps low. This would reduce the 8% nominal pretax return to 6% (8%–2%).

Now we can account for the effects of inflation. Since we pumped up the real rate of 5% to a nominal 8% (to account for inflation), we now have to subtract the 3% from 6% to get back to the real, or inflation-adjusted, rate of return. This brings us to a 3% rate of return after taxes and inflation. This 3% represents the return divided between you and your advisor.

Finally, we come to the effect of the final horseman, fees. The advisor typically charges between 1 and 2%. At this point, 1 or 2%-plus starts to looks pretty significant, since only 3% is available, and we can begin to see the real impact of fees. Over time, the only rate of return that really matters is the after-tax, after-fees real rate of return: we'll call this the *effective* rate of return. Even though we would like to think we're making 8% per year, we really are not. The real question now is the nature of the division of the remaining 3% between you and your advisor. Your advisor might receive an average fee amounting to 1.5% (or possibly more), the same as your effective rate of return. It becomes clear that the advisor will likely be getting about as much as you, or even more return from your capital over the years as you are in real terms. And it's your capital!

It is instructive to look at some other possibilities. If you were to use low-fee index funds, as I suggest, your annual effective rate of return—since the fees range from .1 to, say, .5%—would be at least 2.5% (3%–0.5%), historically, which would be compounded year after year in your account. Not bad, really.

What Are We Getting for Our Fees?

So, now we have an idea of the effects of the fees we are typically paying to advisors. What are we getting in return for the substantial fees we are paying? I feel there are two distinct functions, which should be separated in our minds.

What We All Need and Should Be Paying for: Good Advice from the Well Informed

One function of advisors should be to give good general financial advice. For the large majority of investors, this is a very valuable function. An advisor can help clarify financial goals, encourage saving an adequate amount for retirement, and help navigate the intricacies of the U.S. defined-contribution (DC) retirement system and the tax system. An advisor, ideally, can provide assistance in assembling investments that provide reasonable rates of return, while taking into account the risk tolerance of the individual. It is always good to be able to talk to a knowledgeable advisor

RATE OF RETURN ON INVESTMENT: WHAT IS A REALISTIC MEASURE?

What is a realistic measure of the rate of return on investment? This is the key measure of your investment results; it is the annual percentage by which your nest egg is increasing in value. As is generally the case, it is important to have a clear-eyed assessment of your results rather than accept a rosy but unrealistic interpretation. There are a number of rates frequently encountered, and it seems important to understand just how each is computed. It is also important to base our judgment of our investing success on the most realistic value available. As we account for the various factors diminishing our rates of return (the Deadly Horsemen), the calculated rates become progressively more realistic, but progressively smaller as well.

Nominal rate of return: The annual rate of return we may see quoted, which generally represents the result of the stock dividends, bond interest, and capital gains over a year, may be called the *nominal rate*. This rate, which often seems quite satisfactory to the investor, actually accounts for none of the relevant horsemen conspiring to reduce your actual return rate. It excludes the real-world factors of inflation, taxes, and fees.

Real rate of return: The real rate of return, as described earlier, is corrected for annual inflation. This rate is a more realistic measure than nominal rate. It is more rational to accept the real or inflation-adjusted rate of return, since correction for diminution in the purchasing power of your funds is clearly necessary for a pragmatic assessment.

Change in net asset value (NAV) or portfolio value: When we look at the performance of our investment portfolio or the track records of mutual funds, we will generally see quoted an average change in value over a period of time. These measures include the effects of fees, which must be subtracted from the nominal rates of return on investment.

"Effective" rate of return: If we want to determine just how well our investments are really performing, however, we must account for the effects of all three deadly horsemen that decrement our returns: inflation, taxes, and fees. It is harder to calculate such a rate than the rates described above, since taxes in particular can only be estimated, and fee levels are highly variable among investments vehicles. Nonetheless, it is possible to make reasonable estimates of both taxes and fees, and it is essential to do so if we wish to estimate a realistic "effective" rate of return. I will define the effective rate of return as one accounting for the effects of inflation, taxes, and fees.

While nominal rates of capital gain will be computed for several investment strategies in Chapters 8 and 9, I will ultimately return to and stress the "effective" rate of return as the best benchmark of investment performance in Chapter 15.

when one is considering major purchases and their effects, or to outline the implications of a mortgage or loan. It would seem the vast majority of investors could benefit from such general advice on the management of their assets, and regular periodic updates. Since the typical investor has no or minimal training in such matters, regular consultation with a knowledgeable advisor is a very good idea, and there should likely be a good deal more such interaction, not less.

Additionally, individual investors are confronted by complexities affecting their investing with regard to taxation and the structure and rules for various government-sponsored retirement vehicles, such as 401(k) plans and the variants of IRA plans available. We are trying to keep everything as simple as possible, but the government has set up complex, arguably irrational, and continually changing tax and retirement schemes. An example is the U.S. estate tax, which is an important factor in the financial plans of many: there is a 2009 exclusion amount of $3.5 million, and repeal is scheduled for 2010, but reinstatement is also currently planned in 2011 with only a $1 million exclusion amount. Individual investors can hardly be expected to keep track of such bizarre changes in government policies directly affecting investment decisions. Knowledgeable advisors can be expected to provide valuable assistance to individual investors, and keep them current concerning all these details.

In the best of possible worlds, well-qualified knowledgeable advisors would provide such information and guidance in return for reasonable hourly fees. The services outlined will be of substantial value, meriting substantial compensation paid in this manner.

The Custodial Account: An Excellent Financial Arrangement (for the Advisor)

The second function of an advisor may be to set up and manage your portfolio, generally of stocks and bonds. You've seen from Chapter 4 that the best plan is to allocate your investments between stock index mutual funds, and bond funds. The information available on long-term performance in stock market investing, much of which is summarized in Chapter 4, provides overwhelming evidence of the superiority of this approach.

We might ask if there is any real proof or evidence that investing via an advisor generally leads to enhanced rates of return for individual investors. It turns out that a very large study of rates of return for individuals was conducted for the period from 1996 to 2002, analyzing the performance achieved for individuals working with advisors to choose investments in over 4000 mutual funds, and individuals making such choices on their own. This study was summarized in the publication *Morningstar*[11] by Donald Moine and termed "The Study of the Decade." The surprising result of this large study was that the rates of return (after accounting for all expenses) was over twice as high for individuals working on their own compared to those working with advisors (6.626% vs. 2.924%, respectively).

An obvious follow-up question will be just why individuals working via advisors do not see better performance. The major reasons are well summarized by a former broker recently in the *Toronto Globe and Mail*[12]. Garth Rustand, the confessing ex-broker notes that the key reason is conflict of interest; the broker or advisor who has a choice of investment vehicles will tend to choose those that generate more commissions rather than those that offer the best risk-adjusted rate of return.

"If you're on commission, it's very, very difficult, almost impossible, to do what is best for the client," says Rustand.

Both the latter two publications ("The Study of the Decade" and "What Can an Ex-Broker Teach You? Plenty"[13] are felt particularly revealing and are abstracted in the appendix to this book.

While the above discussion may be eminently reasonable, the large majority of advisors do not function in the manner I suggest. This would involve providing good general financial advice, and advising on investments that you could largely direct yourself, all in exchange for a reasonable hourly fee. The best estimate I have found is that only about 10% function that way[14]. Advisors want you to transfer your funds to a custodial account, for which you are charged an annual fee, typically 1 to 2%.

The reason behind the overwhelming preference for this arrangement on the part of "wealth managers" is that it is much more lucrative for them. It is instructive to consider the management of the wealth of a rather high-income individual in later career; let's say this fortunate person has $1 million to invest. It would seem reasonable that the investor might meet quarterly with the advisor for an hour, and that an additional eight hours might be required per year for meeting preparation and providing ad hoc advice on a variety of issues.

Professionals such as lawyers charge by the hour, and it would certainly seem reasonable for the advisor, as a professional, to charge perhaps $200 per hour for their work. For an average of 2,000 hours worked each year, it works out to $400,000 per annum. We might remember here that the advisor did not have to go to law school or pass the bar, and that there are actually few specific qualifications for this profession[15], so this pay rate does seem reasonable. The annual fees for the year to the investor would thus be about $2,400. If the advisor is capable and gives good advice, this is likely very worthwhile to the investor.

If the manager sets up and manages the custodial account of $1,000,000, what are the fees? If an average fee of 1.5% is charged, the manager will receive $15,000 in fees rather than $2,400. What does the manager of the custodial account do for the much larger fee charged to manage the custodial account? It would perhaps look unseemly to just invest in a handful of low-fee mutual funds (although some wealth managers actually do this—some specialized in Bernie Madoff funds and charged a whopping 2% fee), so the manager generally assembles a stock-and-bond portfolio containing a good many issues. You already know from Chapter 4, however, that it is futile to attempt to provide superior returns this way; this is exactly what the actively managed funds have been doing for years, and overwhelming evidence shows that these funds slightly underperform the market averages. The manager will likely imply that the superiority of the research arm of their firm, combined with their investing acumen, can really provide superior results, but we should know better. We are trying to invest on the basis of the best evidence available, and no substantial evidence of performance superiority will be offered. What the manager is really doing in assembling such a portfolio can be described as creating an illusion of investment productivity. You are likely to be paying dearly for such illusions.

A Better Model for Advisors in the Future?

In the modern era, a durable investment management strategy should be mutually beneficial to the advisor and the client. This is the case in the general model I outline above, in which a knowledgeable advisor provides general financial and investment advice, as well as advice on specific investment allocations.

Since modern investing should be mutual fund–based, the investment allocations could be set up and monitored by the client online, or by the advisor if preferred, all within the payment constraints of an hourly fee. The model of the custodial account managed for a fixed percentage fee, by comparison, seems an anachronism dating back to the days prior to the wide availability of stock index mutual funds, bond funds, and online investing. In the custodial account model, the interests of the advisor and client are not aligned, since the advisor's primary motivation is a high fee structure, which is in conflict with the client's primary goal of a high rate of return.

An attractive alternative would be to decouple the advice component from the investment component, which are combined in the custodial account model. To avoid this custodial model, and to retain the possibility of receiving regular knowledgeable input concerning investing and comprehensive financial advice, there are some options. If one invests through the index funds of large U.S. fund companies such as Fidelity or Vanguard, considerable investing advice is available online and by phone. In some locations, such firms have offices where one can interact directly with an advisor; the level of service is a function of the level of funds in your account.

Although only a minority of advisors appear willing to provide advice on an hourly basis, it may be possible to find one through the National Association of Personal Financial Advisors (http://www.napfa.org). This organization has been existence since 1983, and their mission is to "provide independent financial advice that's not clouded by compensation based on the purchase or sale of a financial product." They advertise that their members provide truly comprehensive fee-only financial advice and planning. This approach would seem to offer a realistic prospect for getting the regular and expert advice needed while avoiding the confines of the custodial account.

When you are looking for an advisor as suggested, always remember what you are looking for, and what should not influence you. You should clearly have a good rapport with the advisor, and the quality of the overall financial planning advice is the key consideration. In particular, the external trappings of a potential advisor should not influence you unduly. There is likely no demonstrable correlation between the quality of the advice or investment acumen with the fine suit, the fashionable office, or (perhaps especially) the winning personality of the potential advisor. Choosing an advisor is a hard-nosed business decision, and you are looking for cost-effective competence.

CHAPTER 6

ONE THING IS CERTAIN: YOU CAN'T TIME THE MARKETS . . .

When one considers techniques for outperforming any particular stock market index, the only two real possibilities are stock selection and market timing. *Market timing* refers to selling when prices are relatively high and buying when they are relatively low. In Chapter 4, a great deal of evidence was presented concerning the ineffectiveness of stock selection. Since the ability to time markets with any degree of consistency would be extremely valuable, it has long been a topic of great interest, and numerous methods for such timing have been proposed. What are the possibilities that market timing might give superior performance?

For opinions as to the general possibility of timing the stock markets, we should perhaps look to advice from leading authorities. Following are comments from three highly respected figures in stock investing. Benjamin Graham wrote *The Intelligent Investor*, a book that was called "by far the best book on investing ever written" by Warren Buffett. John Bogle is the father of the modern stock index fund, and author of several highly respected recent books on stock investing. Burton Malkiel is the author of the classic text on the stock market, *A Random Walk Down Wall Street*. What do these major figures in stock investing think about the possibility of market timing?

> *"The investor can scarcely take seriously the innumerable predictions which appear almost daily and are his for the asking. Yet in many cases he pays attention and even acts on them. Why?"*
>
> *—Benjamin Graham, The Intelligent Investor*[1]

> *"The idea that a bell rings to signal when investors should get into or out of the stock market is simply not credible. After nearly fifty years in this business, I do not know of anybody who has done it successfully and consistently. I don't even know anybody who knows anybody who has done it successfully and consistently."*
>
> *—John C. Bogle, Common Sense on Mutual Funds*[2]

> *"The stock market has no memory. The central proposition of charting is absolutely false, and investors who follow its precepts will accomplish nothing but increasing substantially the brokerage charges they pay."*
>
> *—Burton Malkiel, A Random Walk Down Wall Street*[3]

As if these statements were not enough, literature on stock investing richly details reasons for the failure of market timing techniques. It has also been noted that there have been individuals who have found correlates to stock market movements based on past performance, but none of these have proved successful prospectively[4].

Other critics point out the difficulty and expense of repeatedly getting in and out of the market. In the recent very troubled times in the market, various advisors in the media routinely note that it is foolish to get out of the market, since it is impossible to know the right time to get back in. The general consensus among the large majority of financial advisors and planners is that market timing is simply impossible—no systematic attempts can be made to perform this function.

Should We Accept This Dogma of Impossibility?

I've summarized above the widely held consensus view that market timing is an impossible task; this is clearly the prevailing dogma. It is interesting to consider the implications of this view if indeed it is true. The studies and data summarized in Chapter 4 very clearly indicate the futility of individual stock picking, and the superiority of low-fee stock index fund investing. The great weight of current opinion seems to support the concept that stock market timing is also a futile endeavor. It is perhaps not too difficult to understand this sense of futility, since the record of market timing efforts has typically been so poor. It has been noted, (2-4), that the great majority of such "timing" consists of emotion-driven decisions of individual investors. The general discouragement of prolonged market drops leads to capitulation and selling, whereas the euphoria of extended bull cycles leads most investors to buy near market tops. As will be documented in the next chapter, neither fundamental nor technical market considerations have lead to practical and reliable methods for timing investment decisions.

If it is really true that both stock selection and market timing are not productive activities, the logical conclusion is that the only rational form of stock market investing is a buy-and-hold approach using index funds. There would be no point in efforts either to select stocks or time markets to enhance returns beyond the mean returns of a particular market.

I have indicated that an overriding basic principle of a scheme for personal investment is maximum simplicity, and investing your stock allocation in stock index mutual funds with a buy-and-hold strategy is a very simple approach. It may be your favored approach if you have no interest in a return greater than the general market average.

However, the average investor, on reflection, may not be satisfied with average returns if there is a realistic possibility of superior performance. At the time of writing, with U.S. and world markets at levels similar to those of 12 years ago, the possibility of enhancement of rate of return over the general market seems quite desirable. There are times when it may be advantageous to look beyond the widely held view, and the possibility of enhancement of a rate of return beyond that of the buy-and-hold approach certainly seems worth a look.

Albert Einstein said that "Everything should be made as simple as possible, but not simpler." The approach seems as appropriate for systems of personal investing as for theories of the universe. It would not seem a good idea to go beyond the index fund buy-and-hold approach unless it can be shown that a benefit can be achieved in some way. Although I always favor simplicity, I will next be describing techniques that can be employed to very significantly improve returns beyond buy-and-hold.

A New Approach

The opinions of the experienced market observers quoted above have primarily resulted from observation of the poor records of trading based on general market sentiment, and rather esoteric technical systems applied to individual stock charts. It turns out, however, that with the application of computer-based online technical systems applied to major stock indices and their corresponding funds, we are dealing with an entirely different approach to market timing than that which has gained a well-deserved ill repute.

Major market indices have unique characteristics resulting from their broad and unchanging composition and relatively low volatility, and are uniquely amenable to technical timing techniques that have recently become practical online. These characteristics are quite different from those of individual stocks, and it will be shown that these characteristics allow for effective timing over the longer term, which is a key element of the organized technique for index fund investing that in this book I've named "The System."

In the next six chapters, techniques for timing the purchase and sale of stock index mutual funds will be described, and the enhancement of rates of return using such techniques will be summarized. It will be shown that not only is stock market index timing possible, but it is in fact the only realistic technique for achieving rates of return superior to the general market.

Since the term *market timing* has become so discredited, with reflexive skepticism and derision from most quarters, a new term to describe our efforts in this general area will be useful. In this regard, I use the term *market monitoring* to describe the use of market trend analysis relevant to trading of stock index mutual funds. This new descriptor may lead to less of the visceral disdain associated with attempts to analyze and exploit market trends, and I'll use this term in the following discussions.

CHAPTER 7

. . . OR CAN YOU? TECHNICAL ANALYSIS AS A MARKET TIMING TOOL

If we hope to enhance our investing performance by identifying major stock market trends, we will need to find and exploit some form of analysis which has been proved effective, and which is realistically implementable for the average investor. The two candidates for such an analytic approach are fundamental and technical market analysis.

Fundamental vs. Technical Analysis

Fundamental analysis of a stock or market uses the underlying company and/or economic data, increases in company earnings, and so on that might be expected to affect future security prices. This is the type of analysis used by actively managed mutual funds to analyze individual stocks and create a stock portfolio, for example, as discussed in Chapter 4.

Fundamental analysis has also been applied to the problem of timing overall stock market movements. Likely since the beginning of markets, there have been timing efforts based on efforts to integrate available information on the state of the economy and market levels and prospects, and make predictions as to the probable future course. There are many stock newsletters and market seers in the media who regularly present their opinions as to the most likely future market direction. The record of predictions from such quarters has been highly inconsistent, though, and it is hardly practical to give serious consideration to a market timing strategy based on such intermittent and unreliable pronouncements[1]. It is really not surprising that such advice, coming from an individual trying periodically to integrate a wide range of economic and market data and make a perhaps dramatic announcement of the future market course, will be wrong as often as right.

Technical analysis does not consider such fundamental data, but instead attempts to discern future price action of an individual stock or market using technical rather than fundamental considerations. Such systems may consider only selected and often esoteric technical indicators compiled from a variety of sources. For example, assessment of investor sentiment from surveys may be used as indicators of the overall market's future direction. Paradoxically, a surplus of bullish sentiment is generally taken as a negative indicator, the theory being that bullish sentiment is most pronounced when the market is near a peak. Other technical systems employ graphically based techniques, in which stock or stock market patterns as revealed by charting are used to predict future price trends.

So we have two possible approaches to attempting to outperform the general stock market: fundamental analysis, which seeks to analyze a stock or market's economic underpinnings, and technical analysis, which ignores these factors and uses technical aids in an effort to predict future stock and market movements. Intuitively, it likely seems a lot more credible that fundamental analysis should be capable of selecting the best stocks, and possibly to determine future overall market prospects, leading to superior performance over time. The technical approach likely seems rather odd, and one in fact may get the feeling that technical analysts of the stock market may represent something of an eccentric group, if not a lunatic fringe[2].

As we have seen in Chapter 4, however, data concerning the possibility of outperforming the market by fundamental analysis and stock selection indicates unequivocally that such an approach is unproductive in attaining a market edge. Similarly, as noted above, fundamental analysis is not proved useful in analyzing overall stock market trends.

The bottom line? If we want to outperform the overall stock market, technical analysis for market timing remains our only potentially viable option, so we should examine this possibility closely.

Examples of Purely Technical Systems

In Chapter 2, the technical system reviewed each week on W$W, the most popular program on investing in the history of television, was mentioned. This system, created by respected analyst Robert Nurock, was a compilation of ten general technical indicators that had shown some correlation in the past with general stock market trends[3]. The overall output was obtained by assigning each of the ten indicators a +1, neutral, or –1 value, respectively indicating bullish, neutral, and bearish future market prospects. If the overall sum was positive, the indication was for a market uptrend; if negative, a downtrend was indicated. A net balance of +5 was needed for a buy signal, and a net balance of –5 indicated a sell signal.

I am a long-time subscriber to the *New York Times*, and for years, a plot of "put/call ratio," (Figure 7-1) was printed in the business pages of this venerable newspaper as their sole "technical" indicator of the likely future direction of the U.S. stock market. A put is an option to sell a

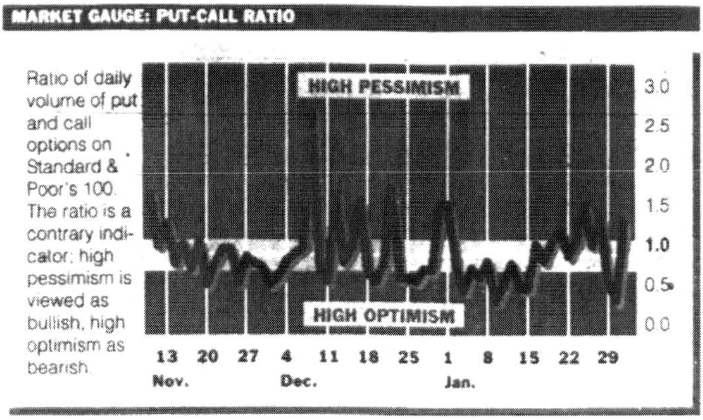

Figure 7-1: Plot of the put/call ratio. Higher values of the ratio indicated pessimism, which was interpreted as bullish, and vice versa.

Source: *The New York Times*. Business Section. February 1, 2001

given stock at a stated price over a given length of time and a call is a similar option to buy. If substantially more investors were buying puts (hoping the market would go down) than calls (hoping the market would go up), the put/call ratio would be high, and market sentiment was indicated to be pessimistic. As indicated above, though, the counterintuitive interpretation of pessimistic market sentiment is that the market is more likely to go up than down. The general concept is that the pessimists dominating the market have already sold stocks, and the market is poised for an upswing.

Both the W$W technical index and the put/call ratio are examples of purely technical indicators used to assess the general future direction of the market. It's important to consider that these latter two indicators were considered state-of-the-art for technical analysis, and presented as such to a wide audience in the print and television media. The indicators were important features for quite a while in the media in which they appeared, among the most prominent in the country: the most successful U.S. television show in history on the stock market, and the business pages of a leading American newspaper.

The Justification for Such Technical Indicators

With the benefit of hindsight, we might consider the initial justification for the use of these technical indicators, their ultimate fates, and the likely effects of the advocacy of these and similar indicators over the years. While both the W$W index and the put/call ratio were typical tools used by technical analysts at the time, the reasoning behind their use was never very clearly articulated. If one wrote to the W$W show, a description of the ten indicators would be provided, but an explanation as to just why the system should work was lacking, and never really provided on the show itself. Similarly, there was no real explanation as to why the put/call ratio might be a valuable technical tool other than the thought that high pessimism is viewed as bullish, and high optimism as bearish.

An even more important consideration than the lack of a coherent justification for the use of these indicators was the lack of a clearly documented demonstration of their practical use in market timing, particularly in relatively recent times. What should have been required before promulgating such indicators was a demonstration of just when the indicators gave clear signals to buy or sell stocks, and whether it has been proved possible to profit over the general market by using these signals. This is really the bottom line for an indicator; it is not enough simply to provide some vague indication of general market sentiment.

Such a compilation seems absolutely necessary; the enhancement of rate of return achievable with the indicators (if any) should have been clearly documented and presented for such indicators to have credibility. Ideally, each time the indicator was presented, the most recent indicated position (long or short) should have been indicated, along with a summary of recent success or failure of utility of the indicator. This omission of any such assessments seems remarkable, since it would seem any intelligent viewer or reader would be most interested in the past record of sell/buy indications, and the nature and date of the latest overall recommendation.

The Fates of These Indicators

As to the histories of these two widely followed indicators, the W$W index was presented each week from 1970, as part of the initial summary of weekly market activity. The use of the index, in the form described above, was discontinued in 1989 after an on-air clash between Lou Rukeyser and Robert Nurock, the analyst who originally formulated the index. The put/call plot was dropped from the business pages of the *New York Times* without explanation some years ago.

The widespread lack of credibility of technical analysis is probably not difficult to understand if we consider the widespread dissemination of the W$W index and put/call ratio, along with similar indicators, as the best available technical tools over many years. In the end, their practical utility in market timing was never convincingly demonstrated, and both indicators were both ultimately discarded without ceremony. It seems very likely that the reputation of technical market analysis in general has been largely determined by the success or failure of such technical indicators, presented so prominently to the general public over the years. If these were the best tools that the analysts could come up with, why should any attention be paid to technical analysis at all?

If we are to consider the use of technical systems for market timing, perhaps we can learn something from the experience with the technical systems described above, and articulate some criteria for judging the utility of any such systems considered for use in the future. Firstly, there should be a clear rationale for the use of a particular parameter; it could be of use in market trend–following or provide some proved indicator of market sentiment, for example. Even more important, clear-cut documentation of past utility over a relevant period of time in the past must be shown. It is hard to see why future utility should be expected of parameters for which there had been no clearly documented past record of success. In considering the use of any technical parameter in the future, the rationale for use and historic record of enhancing rates of return must be clearly known and stated.

Another critical characteristic for a useful market indicator is, simply, simplicity. Not only may one have difficulty understanding a complex indicator presented once a week, such as the W$W index, but one is also forced to rely on the creators of the index for their regular readings. Ideally, a useful indicator would be easy to understand, simple to determine, and available to an individual investor on a daily basis.

Graphically Based Technical Systems for Market Timing

Graphical or chart-based systems attempt to assess the likely future course of a stock or stock market based on past patterns of price movements. There is an extensive literature on this subject. Much of it deals with analysis of individual stock data, and may not be directly relevant to our goal of investing via stock market index funds. There are some

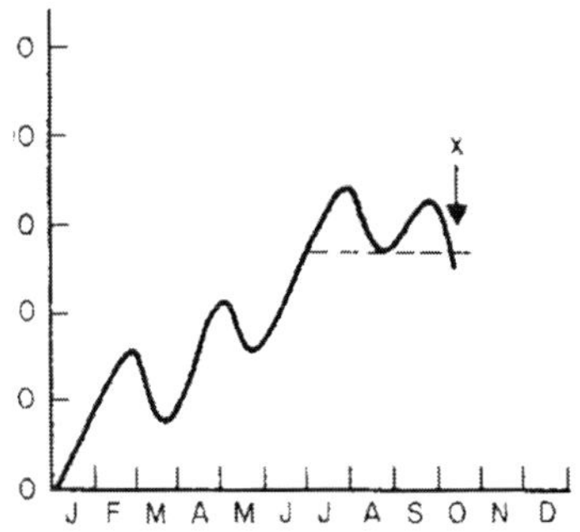

Figure 7-2: The uptrend pattern of market movements can be thought of as a series of successively higher peaks and troughs. When a new peak and trough are lower than the last peak/trough pair, a market reversal is indicated (at point x), where the prior uptrend reverts to a downtrend.

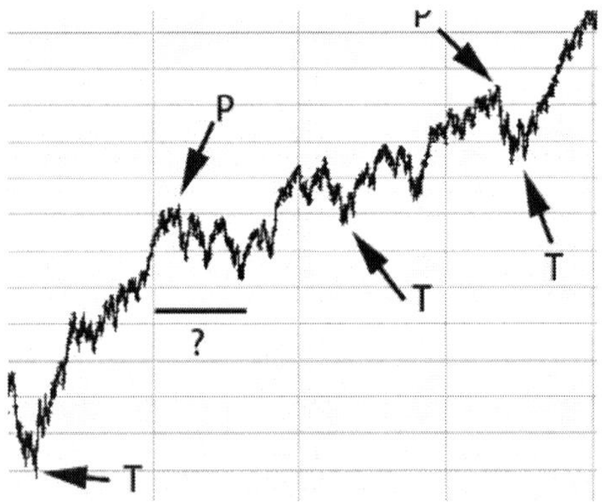

Figure 7-3: Real stock market data (S&P 500 Average, 2003 through 2007). The pattern of successively higher peaks (P) and troughs (T) is seen, but the data is much noisier than in the model. The region indicated (?) in 2004 contains several successively lower peaks and troughs. Is this a sell signal? All graphical techniques using pattern recognition tend to present considerable ambiguity.

Source: (Figure 7-2)Pring, M.J. 1980. Technical Analysis Explained. New York: Mc-Graw-Hill Pring; Technical analysis explained (Figure 7-3) from Internet plot of sp500 using BigCharts.

valuable lessons from consideration of some types of graphical systems that have been applied to market indices in the past, however.

Dow Theory

The general approach of looking to prior stock price movements to see whether patterns might be evident that would have the potential to indicate future market trends goes back at least to the work of Charles Dow, author of the Dow theory of market movements[4], originally published in a series of *Wall Street Journal* editorials from 1900 to 1902. In its simplest form, the theory considers market uptrends as consisting of a series of successively higher stock price peaks and troughs (Figure 7-2) and market downtrends as a series of successively lower peaks and troughs.

In rationalizing such movements, an uptrend may be considered a situation in which an excess of demand for a stock results in upward price movements, which alternate with periods of consolidation when an equilibrium is reached and retrenchment in price occurs, leading to a trough following a peak. If excess demand then continues to persist, the characteristic shape of successively higher peaks and troughs is seen, as shown. A trend reversal occurs when the pattern changes—when a successive peak and trough fall at lower levels than the preceding peak/trough pair. This situation indicates the start of a downtrend, and the pattern and reasoning behind its occurrence are simply the converse of that seen in an uptrend.

It is interesting to note that real markets are in fact well represented in almost all cases by this general model, as shown. If one looks at graphs of yearly, weekly, daily or even hourly stock market data, the same general patterns are evident. Uptrends are a series of higher troughs and peaks, and downtrends a series of lower troughs and peaks.

Dow theory has been successfully used to analyze stock price and stock index movements in many reported studies[5]. In a modern update to Dow theory[6] by Jack Schannep, the results of applying Dow theory to the Dow Jones Industrial Average were determined for data from 1954 to 2000. One would only own the Dow stocks when an upturn was indicated by Dow theory, and be out of the market when a downturn was expected. An increase in rate of return from 8.1% (using the buy-and-hold strategy) was improved to 8.9% using Dow theory, with trades in or out of the market only required every year or two on the average.

The Dow technique might be called a pattern recognition technique in that analysis of price movements involves the recognition of patterns of price movements associated with trends and trend reversals. Such recognition may allow one to buy and sell near market lows and highs, respectively. Quite a number of pattern recognition techniques have been used over the years as tools for market timing; a "head and shoulders" configuration has been described, for instance, as characteristic of a market top.

Such techniques have proved useful, at least in some hands, in market timing, but pattern recognition techniques all tend to give signals (telling when to buy or sell stocks), which often seem quite ambiguous. In the real world of investing, or course, we are always doing our analysis at the extreme "right edge" of the chart, and really have no idea of the rest of the story.

In the diagrammatic representation of Dow theory in bull and bear markets in Figure 7-2, the general upward trend trend is quite clear. In the real data of price movements on the right (Figure 7-3), however, it is not really clear if a series of relatively smaller and lower peaks and troughs really represent the emergence of a downtrend. This is but one example of the ambiguity often present in the interpretation of such graphical pattern recognition techniques, which involve quite a bit of art as well as science.

What Is Really Required for Practical Market Timing (Monitoring)?

What is really required is a technique that can be used to analyze price data consistently over time, and output unambiguous signals that do not require interpretation of complex patterns of price movements. The realization of such a tool would lead essentially to a technique for analyzing market data in a consistent, automated way, giving indications of the most likely course of the future market direction. To show promise, such a system would have to be shown to be effective in providing such indications over a substantial period of time to provide an adequate historical basis for its utility.

Such systems have in fact been developed, and have been proved effective in timing certain markets.

The Zweig/Davis Market Timing Model

Martin Zweig, in his popular book on the stock market *Winning on Wall Street*, describes a system of market timing based not on pattern recognition techniques, but on a rather simple quantitative model[7]. This technique involves buying (a buy signal) when the market rises at least 4% from its lowest recent value, and a sell signal is given if the market falls at least 4% from a recent high. Mr. Zweig and his partner Ned Davis showed that this straightforward technique could be very effective in timing some markets, providing much higher annualized returns than a simple buy-and-hold strategy.

When applied to the Value Line Composite Index (an unweighted average of the stock prices listed in the Value Line Investment Survey) from 1966 to 1982, the technique detected a total of roughly 100 buy or sell signals, or about 6 per year. The bottom line was that, using this system in this market, an annual rate of return averaging 14.9% could be generated—more than 12% better than a buy-and-hold strategy. In the second edition of his book (1997), Zweig applied exactly the same 4% model to analyze the returns that might be obtained using this strategy as compared to buy-and-hold. In this analysis, the trial was extended to 30 years right up to 1996. The results were very similar to the previous analysis (Table 7-1): the timing system was successful in outperforming buy-and-hold by over 10%.

In spite of the general feeling that market timing systems do not work, the Zweig/Davis analysis would appear to indicate that not only can a trend-following system work in greatly outperforming a buy-and-hold strategy based on retrospective data (as we see in the 1986 edition of the book), but that such a system seems capable of prospective success in predicting similar benefits in the future (as documented in the 1997 edition[8]).

The success of the system described by Zweig and Davis represents something of a breakthrough compared to earlier technical efforts for

Zweig/Davis Trading System Performance		
Period	1966–1988	1966–1996
Rate of return with system	+14.9%	+13.3%
Return with buy-and-hold	+2.4%	+3.2%

Table 7-1: Zweig/Davis system summary table: The rate of return using the system for the Value Line Composite for the two time periods studied greatly exceeds that attained with a simple buy-and-hold strategy.

several reasons. The system gives buy and sell signals that are unambiguous, in contrast to a rather large number of other chart-based techniques, which rely on rather subjective signals based on pattern recognition. The whole system can be readily implemented using a calculator or computer as a tool for daily analysis and automated, dispassionate generation of buy and sell signals. The enhanced rate of return is impressive, as is the continued success over a 30-year period.

Some Problems with the Zweig/Davis System

While Zweig's approach has been very successful, there are some features of his methods that might give us pause. A major issue for any stock market timing technique is that, if it is to be useful to an individual investor, it should be quite easy to implement and result in relatively few trades. While the proposed technique based on stock market movements could be implemented in theory by an investor, keeping track of the 4% thresholds and so on over time would require a fair bit of daily attention and calculations. Also, there are a great many trades (about six per year) created by Mr. Zweig's technique, and only about half are profitable.

The reason the technique works, of course, are that many small losses are created, and a few large gains. This particular system also seems to work well only for market indices that are unweighted—that is, not weighted in the index in a manner proportional to the capitalization of the individual stocks. As will be discussed below, the market indices of most interest to us as investors turn out to be the more ubiquitous indices such as the S&P 500 Average, which are weighted by the market capitalization of the component stocks. It is these indices that are tracked by many low-fee stock index mutual funds, which are the best vehicles for stock market investing, as discussed in Chapter 4.

Another problem for practical use in market timing is that, using the Zweig/Davis system for market timing, the rate of return is enhanced greatly by alternating between long and short positions in the market. In order to short a market, one generally has to sell shares lent to them by a brokerage firm, and buy them back at a later date, hopefully after the shares have decreased in value. A possible mechanism to implement the Zweig/Davis trading system would be via futures for the Value Line Index, which are listed on the Kansas City Board of Trade. For the average investor, however, neither of these techniques can be recommended due to their complexity and the high degree of risk involved, especially with index futures. A more easily implemented, less risky mechanism would seem required for real-world implementation by the average investor for successful "market monitoring."

CHAPTER 8

A TECHNIQUE FOR TRADING THE S&P 500 AVERAGE INDEX FUNDS

As indicated in Chapter 6, the prevailing perspective in the investment world is that one simply cannot "time" stock market purchases and sales, in an effort to increase rate of return, with any degree of consistency. It was noted that the buy-and-hold approach to index fund investing has the virtue on remarkable simplicity, but would we really be content with buy-and-hold if we felt that there was a realistic chance for better performance using some practical timing mechanism?

The economist John Kenneth Galbraith noted that "the conventional view serves to protect us from the painful job of thinking." Perhaps a little painful thinking can lead us to a more profitable future than that dictated by the most widespread current investment strategies.

Development of a Trading Technique for U.S. Stock Indices and Related Mutual Funds

The goal for successful market timing (we'll use the term "market monitoring") is to define a system for finding longer-term trends in stock prices, and provide clear indications, or signals, to buy into the stock market relatively early in these longer-term uptrends, and then to exit when a longer-term downtrend is identified. I started thinking about the possibility of having a system for market monitoring after I (along with many others) experienced some painful financial reverses during the substantial drop in U.S. and other markets' equity prices from mid-2000 to 2002.

It was clear that the buy-and-hold approach did not seem to be working any more. On the basis of a number of excellent recent books on the subject[1], and as discussed in Chapter 4, the only form of stock market investment that has seemed to make sense was via the use of low-fee stock funds based on stock market index mutual funds. Such funds provide the critical advantages of excellent diversification, very low management and trading costs, superior long-term performance, and tax efficiency, as we have seen.

If the use of a limited number of major market index funds could be combined with an effective market monitoring system, it would result in the development of a powerful system for personal investment, concerned only with the monitoring of broad market averages such as the S&P 500 Average.

There are number of features of an effective and practical system for index fund investing incorporating a market monitoring system.

1. The system would have to be capable of providing indicators, or signals, to purchase or sell, based on major market indices such

as the S&P 500 Average and possibly other important national and international indices. Since the prices of a number of low-fee mutual funds rise and fall in tandem with these market indices, the indications to buy or sell (signals) would be directly applicable to the trading of index funds.

2. The monitoring system would have to take advantage of the major parts of broad upward market trends occurring over periods of years, while avoiding the bulk of any future severe retreats. The system would not attempt to provide trading signals over the shorter term of weeks or months, but would attempt to discern longer bull or bear markets persisting for a year or several years. There are several important reasons for this longer-term approach: firstly, there would be relatively few trades, making the system simpler and easier to follow. Much less attention over time would be required for such a system compared to one that provided many signals over time.

   Secondly, the tax consequences would be much more favorable. Not only will there be fewer taxable "events" with fewer trades, but if a substantial number of the gains were longer term (longer than one year), the much lower capital gain tax rates would apply to trading profits. Additionally, although trading funds in a family of mutual funds between stock funds and money market or bond funds can be performed at no cost, or relatively low cost, transaction costs can add up in some trading situations, and the fewer trades, the lower the overall trading fees will be.

3. The system should use online stock index data and technical analysis techniques (described below), which are now widely available at a wide range of websites for no charge. This was a necessary

criterion, since only such an arrangement can provide a current analysis of a specific market/fund price direction on a regular basis.

4. The mechanics of the system should be as simple as possible consistent with successful indication of a market's likely future direction. If a technique is pretty good at monitoring markets, but requires significant daily data entry and computation, it will not work for the average investor. On the other hand, if a feature of the analysis is truly necessary for successful trading, it must be retained.

The first issue is just which market index, on which index funds are based, to analyze in order to determine how analysis might help identify major price trends. There are many major indices we see quoted in the media on a daily basis, including the NASDAQ composite index, the Dow Jones Industrial Average, and the S&P 500 Average. The S&P 500 Average is an obvious choice for the U.S. market, since the stocks in the average represent a diverse mix of stocks representing about 75% of the capitalization of U.S. markets[2]. As noted in Chapter 4, there are many low-fee index funds based on this average, including several from Fidelity and Vanguard, with MERs of from .07 to .15%.

Since it seems that an effective market monitoring system for the S&P 500 Average would be very valuable, we'll look at just how this might be done, and what the results of such a system might be over the years compared to a buy-and-hold strategy.

How Far Back Should We Look?

The next question is how far back we should go in analyzing the movements of the S&P 500. It might seem best go back as far as possible, if we want to make sure that the performance of any system to time the market has been consistent over long periods. If we investigate the movements of the S&P 500 Average, along with the daily volume of trading over the past 58 years, we get the following plot.

Looking back over the years, it does appear that the character of U.S. stock market movements has changed considerably over time. Until the later 1980s, and especially prior to 1995, the market didn't show the pattern of

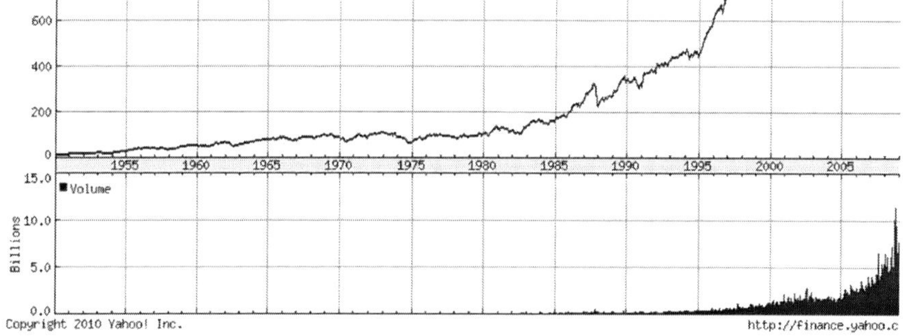

Figure 8-1: Plot of the Standard and Poor's 500 Average since 1950. Since about 1995, the market has shown quite wide price swings compared to earlier periods.

larger prices swings that we see more recently, and the volume of trading was relatively low. Since 1995, however, there really does seem to have been a significant change in the character of the market; the range of variation over time has greatly increased, and the volume of trading has increased substantially. The question then arises, which market time period do we want to analyze as a likely guide to future market movements?

If the character of the market as seen in figure 8-1 were basically the same, analyzing all the way back to 1950 would seem reasonable. Perhaps we would want to go back even further; stock index data for the U.S. market can be found for periods of over 100 years; should we base a modern-day strategy on data back 25, 50, or 100 years? I feel that the dynamics of the markets in much earlier periods are not likely to be of relevance to modern markets. The most relevant period to analyze in predicting future price movements is likely the past 14 years since 1995, since the characteristics of the market seem rather consistent.

One can speculate as to why the more recent market appears to have a different character than in the past: market movements may have been exaggerated by increased use of market derivatives; the world has seen more economic turmoil in recent years, and perhaps the effects of globalization and increased market participation have played roles. Technical analysis that is effective in aiding trading decisions in the past 14 years is unlikely to be effective in the earlier era, and vice versa, given the distinct characteristics of market movements in these periods.

One only has to look at the plot of prices from 1995 onward to see that major long term trends lasting for years have been present. The question is how to identify such long term trends in order to increase our returns.

The Mechanics of the Monitoring System

The goal of our monitoring system is to identify long-term (lasting at least a year) trends among the noise of seemingly random fluctuations that surround the trend. In order to do this, one needs a tool for smoothing out the rather chaotic changes in stock market prices over time. In line with the idea of using as simple a system as possible, it has made sense to investigate stock price daily moving averages (MAs). The simple moving average is the most straightforward tool available, and one that has been used for decades for smoothing stock price data.

Using Moving Averages to Generate Signals

The ability of the moving average approach to provide a more orderly plot, which effectively lags major price trends a bit due to its retrospective nature, has been appreciated for some time. There haven't been, however, a lot of successful published efforts to exploit such plots in a systematic way to develop a system to anticipate future price trends of major U.S. stock markets. One suggestion has been to plot the 200-day moving averages of a price index, to buy into the market when the index or stock price (usually the daily price) path crosses the path of the 200-day average[3], and to sell when the converse occurs. A better approach, however, is to disregard the daily prices themselves and rely only on the longer-term moving averages, which are stabler and less subject to the rather chaotic movements seen in daily index prices.

One straightforward approach is to find an appropriate moving average interval and to determine a buy signal to be the reversal of a neutral or downward trend in the average to an upward trend in the average itself.

In other words, if an upward trend in the plot of the moving average plot begins, this indicates a buy signal. So, a buy signal is given when the slope or trend becomes positive following a negative or neutral trend. Similarly, a sell signal would occur when a positive or neutral trend of moving averages over time becomes a negative trend.

It should be appreciated that the creation of too many trading signals over time will seriously impact the practical application of a market monitoring technique. More trades than absolutely required will tend to limit the possibility of long-term capital gains and their much more favorable tax treatment. Unnecessary trades may also generate additional transaction costs.

If one uses a single moving average, it is difficult to determine a single moving-average value that will allow optimal buy and sell signals without creating too many trading signals.

Using Multiple MAs Simultaneously Works Best

While there are quite a number of possibilities for moving average graphical analysis of stock market price movements at various Internet sites, the goal is to find the simplest possible approach that works. It is quite standard at the various websites to allow the simultaneous plotting of two, three, or even more averages in such an effort. As noted in the description of moving average calculations, the trends up or down in the plots of moving averages depend on the number of days averaged (see sidebar). We can also see that the price variation over time is best considered a composite of trends lasting over variable periods, from days to months. Since we may examine trends over variable periods of time using more than one moving average simultaneously, perhaps this will be a better approach than relying on trends depicted only by one moving average. There is a great deal of variability in both the magnitude of price movements and the periods of time over which these occur. By using several moving averages in tandem, we may find a technique that takes into account the variability, and unpredictability, of these differing time periods over which market movements occur.

In the end, empiric testing of various periods to use multiple averages is required to arrive at a satisfactory technique based on past performance. It turns out that when we look at various possibilities, very good results for indices of interest over the past 14 years can be obtained using the three moving averages of 60, 120, and 210 days combined in a specific way.

In using the three averages, a signal to get in or out of the stock market is indicated only when the trends indicated by *all* of the three averages indicate a change in the overall trend simultaneously. In using three simultaneous averages, we are essentially requiring that the random stock movements over three distinct periods are all pointing in the same direction, minimizing unnecessary signals. Spurious signals resulting from random changes seen over only one time period will be "checked" by the signals over another time period, and *signals will be indicated only when all three agree.*

I'll outline the system I have used for using online stock market index and fund data online to monitor markets and generate signals over time. Although the signals could be called "buy" and "sell" signals, they might better be called "in" and "out" signals, since in their application I will be recommending either having a designated percentage of your capital in stocks, or being entirely out of the stock market, with all your capital in bond funds. The vehicles I recommend for bond investment were outlined in Chapter 4, and these, or money market funds, are where we should park our funds while we wait for the next indication that the time is right to get back into the market.

SMOOTHING STOCK MARKET DATA WITH MOVING AVERAGES

The moving average (MA) is simply the average price at a given point in time, over a fixed prior period of time. The prices averaged are typically the final price at the end of a given day, week, or month. In order to calculate a 20-day moving average, for example, one simply computes the average end-of-day price for the last 20 days. Online tools are available at many websites that allow for the calculation of this *simple* moving average for individual stock, or stock market index data. A great many other methods of analysis, including *exponential* moving averages, which weigh recent data more strongly, are also available, but in keeping with our goal of maximum simplicity, we'll stick with the simple moving averages. Probably the best way to think about market average data over time is as a rather noisy or chaotic variation in price level over variable, unpredictable periods of time. If one wishes to smooth out the data to display market movement over relatively short periods of time, averaging over relatively few days can be performed. To see longer-term market trends, averaging price data over a greater number of days will provide the desired result. In the graph on the right (Figure 8-2), 10-, 50-, and 200-day moving averages are plotted for S&P 500 Average data over a nine-month period (February 1 to November 1, 2007).

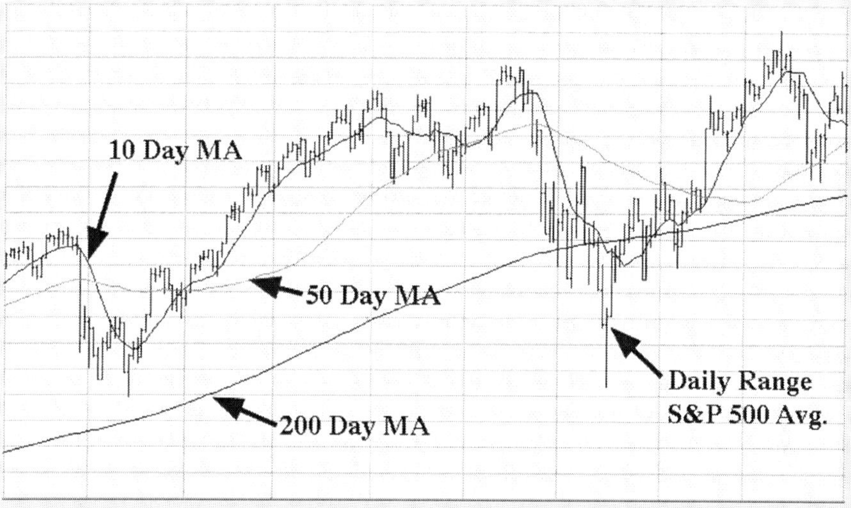

Figure 8-2: The graph above shows that there is the least smoothing for the 10-day average and the most for the 200-day average. The actual stock market data (S&P 500 February 1 to November 1, 2007) has substantial variability over any time period in which we might be interested, and in addition to its great variability, the 10-day average movements up or down often appear to reflect price changes occurring over periods of only a few days. The 50-day average is stabler, and changes over at least weekly periods are reflected in the trends up or down in this average. The least variable 200-day average uptrend is not reversed by the price variations, but continues upward over all 9 months. The longer the period over which the average is taken, the greater the degree of smoothing, and longer the periods of market variation over which market up- or downtrends are indicated.

Starting with the S&P 500 Average, the trading techniques will be illustrated using charts showing daily price movements and the times when "in" and "out" signals are given. The history of transactions and results over the years will be summarized in tables following the charts showing the dates and results of trading.

Using Free Online Market Analysis Tools

In discussions of the online implementation of the monitoring technique, I'll try my best to be detailed and not leave out any steps. I have noted that many descriptions of computer-based techniques suffer from lack of adequate documentation.

There are a great many resources freely available online with which one can chart and analyze stock, mutual fund, and stock index information over time. Many of these websites have decades of historical information available, and can be used to evaluate historical price movements for daily, weekly, or monthly data using a variety of mathematical techniques. While major investment firms all have variants of such charting and analysis techniques at their sites, and such search sites as Google and Yahoo have excellent charting tools, I have used a site called BigCharts primarily. This site is a service of MarketWatch, which is in turn run by Dow Jones, which also publishes the *Wall Street Journal* and *Barron's* magazine. The URL for BigCharts is http://bigcharts.marketwatch.com.

If you enter the BigCharts site, the initial screen will present a number of options for charting/analysis; you should click on the red "Advanced Chart" option from this screen. You will be presented with a new screen with a control panel on the left, which governs the display of a chart that you will create to the right. I've duplicated the control panel in Figure 8-4 to indicate the major items to enter to create the type of chart I have used to trade. You can enter the symbol of the index, stock, or fund of interest in the top white box. In the figure, "SP500" is the symbol for the S&P 500 Average index. Symbols for individual stocks, mutual funds, and stock indices may be found in a number of ways, but perhaps the simplest is just to Google the name of the stock or fund; you should get a number of hits showing the symbol. Symbols for many funds have five letters; in addition to finding the symbols with search engines, you can find them directly at the websites for the mutual fund family to which the fund belongs.

The first parameter to enter is the length of time over which you want to analyze daily price data for the selected stock index or mutual fund. When analyzing the data for the studies I've presented below, I entered "1 month," when actually looking for a signal on a given day. In creating the illustrative plots of trends for longer periods, the desired time period can be entered using the "Custom" time frame option. As to the other entry items, you can compare an entry to an index, fund, or stock of your choosing under "compare to," but you can leave this blank.

Clicking on "indicators" allows us to calculate and display the parameters we will be using to create market trading signals. To use the system, choose (SMA [Simple Moving Average] 3-line) under "Moving Averages," and enter "60, 120, 210" in the box to the right to select 60-, 120-, and 210-day moving averages. There are several ways of displaying the daily market prices, and I have used the default display of price open, high, low, and close (OHLC). The only other entry I suggest is to choose under "Chart Style" the "Big" charts. (I like my charts as big as possible to see things clearly.) When you have entered all the parameters, just click on the red "Draw Chart" button.

It's important to stress that if you wish to used such an online graphical system as a basis for market monitoring, basing the method on

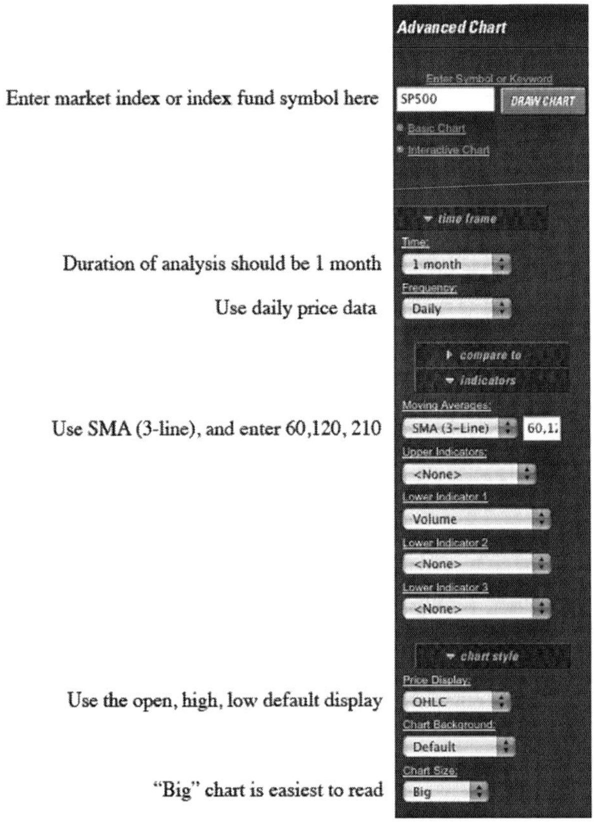

Figure 8-3 Summary of entries used in online analysis of the S&P 500 Average using BigCharts advanced analysis option.

historical results, you must set up and perform the analysis in exactly the same manner to analyze current trends as has been used to provide the original analysis of past data. Only in this manner can you be sure that a system that has worked well in the past will be accurately applied to current market dynamics.

In particular, if you choose a longer display period than one month, the display of moving average trends will change somewhat, since the moving average trend changes are displayed to a lower resolution. Even a different price display than the default open, high, low, and close (OHLC) option will slightly change the display of moving average prices trends. It seems unfortunate that the graphical technique has to be used so consistently and exactly, but it becomes necessary if we are to exploit the power and convenience of free online analysis.

The signals for trading, indicated on the graphs showing the S&P 500 Average from 1995 to 2009, plotted along with the 60-, 120-, and 210-day moving averages, are shown. Some more detailed examples of signals, and the utility of the three moving average approaches will then be presented, and a summary chart showing the dates and results of the indicated trading follows.

While the summary plots (Figures 8-6 and 8-9) are illustrative of the movements of the index price and moving averages, the actual trading decisions were always performed using only the one-month display, allowing resolution of the individual days in the month.

Examples of "IN" and "OUT" signals are shown in Figures 8-7 and 8-8 using the one-month display. Here we see the first indication for buying S&P 500 Index funds on January 27, 1995, followed by the next signal—to sell these funds on October 11, 2000. These month-long plots show (faintly) the range of S&P 500 Index closing prices on each day of the month, and the moving average (MA) plots of the S&P 500 Index for periods of 60, 120, and 210 days. The trends in each MA plot (up or down) are indicated by up or down arrows placed on the appropriate MA plot. Each time the trend changes for any MA, three arrows indicating the three MA trends are placed on the MA plots. The key point to remember is that the overall trend (up or down) is reversed *only when all three trends agree.* In other words, an uptrend (signifying "IN" the market) is reversed only when all three trends, as indicated by the trend arrows, are all in the same upward direction at the same time.

USING THREE MOVING AVERAGES SIMULTANEOUSLY

Why are three moving averages used instead of just one or two, and how were the moving average lengths chosen? Since we are interested only in relatively long-term trends in index mutual fund prices, the moving averages used to provide trading signals must be relatively long. As shown below (Figure 8-4), the 60-, 120-, and 210-day MAs used correspond to periods from almost three months long to almost ten months long. The daily data we are using, of course, is only from those days when markets are open, so weekends and holidays are excluded.

The daily price changes of stock indices can be regarded as noise, but if one views the price history over longer periods of time, there are clearly continuing long-term trends around which price swings lasting weeks to months occur. Since the variation in these swings is completely unpredictable, it is best to use several moving averages of varying length to "sample" the swings, and provide independent indications of the market's current direction. The requirement for a unanimous agreement of all three MAs to indicate a trend tends to prevent unnecessary trades. The indication of a great many trades, many of which result in losses, would tend to render a monitoring system quite impractical.

The theory does indeed work well in practice. A cursory inspection of the graphs of the S&P 500 over 14 years might lead one to suspect that trends indicated that just one average—the 210-day MA—might be used effectively. When one actually performs the analysis, however, one finds many instances in which the use of multiple MAs reduces the number of trades and enhances return.

A compelling example of the need to use multiple MAs will be presented in Chapter 9.

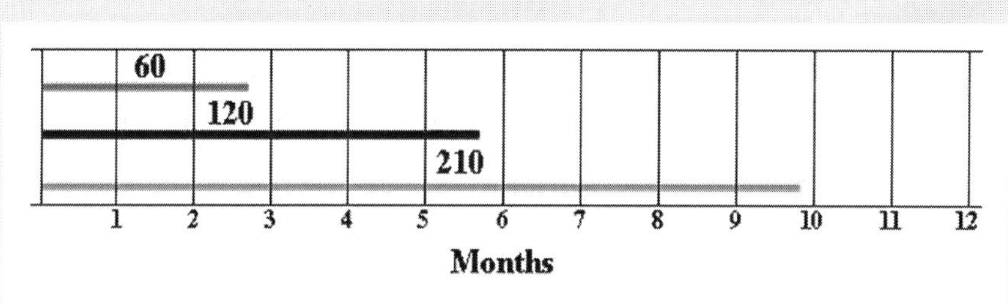

Figure 8-4 Time and month over which the three moving averages were obtained.

UNDERSTANDING THE CHARTS AND CHART SYMBOLS

The charts of the S&P 500 Average over two 7-year periods (Figures 8-6 and 8-9) demonstrate market movements over a 14-year span, and the annotation of the "in" and "out" signals demonstrates the timeliness and infrequency of these signals. While one can grasp the general concept of using multiple moving averages using these charts, it is not possible accurately to determine just when these signals occur in the two 7-year plots. The 1-month plots of the first "IN" and "OUT" signals (Figures 8-7 and 8-8) demonstrate just how these signals are generated. The symbols used to display price data in these latter month-long charts may be unfamiliar to many. The annotation of the individual moving average data also likely requires some description. Both these chart features are illustrated in the chart below. The daily price data, shown only for day 6 in Figure 8-5, is in the default open, high, low, and close (OHLC) format. This is a standard technique for plotting stock and index price data, and is the default option for BigCharts. The manner of depiction of open, high, low, and closing prices is indicated in the example price data for day 6. Since it may be rather difficult to distinguish the three moving averages and evaluate trends in these data, some further annotation beyond that provided by BigCharts has been added. The number of days used to calculate each moving average plot are printed directly through a portion of each plot. In the example, a 60-day moving average is indicated. Since the changes in moving average trends may be difficult to see, a large arrowhead pointing up or down has been added through each moving average plot each time the trend changes direction. In the example below, the trend is initially neutral, but a downtrend is indicated on day 4; this is reversed to an uptrend on day 8. In the plots of real data, remember that all three MA trends must be in agreement to indicate a new overall trend, resulting in an "in or "out" signal.

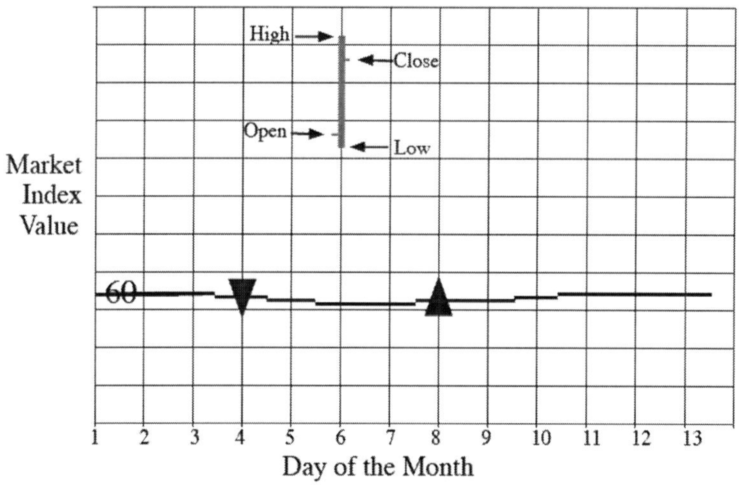

Figure 8-5: Summary of entries used in online analysis of the S&P 500 Average using BigCharts advanced analysis option.

Figure 8-6: S&P 500 Average from 1995 to 2002, with 60- (▲), 120- (■) and 210- (●) day moving averages providing "IN" and "OUT" signals on January 27, 1995, and Oct 11, 2000, respectively. The details of the signals to enter and exit the market are shown in the monthly plots of the S&P 500 and moving average trendlines, (which correspond to the two rectangular regions indicated on this plot) on the following pages.

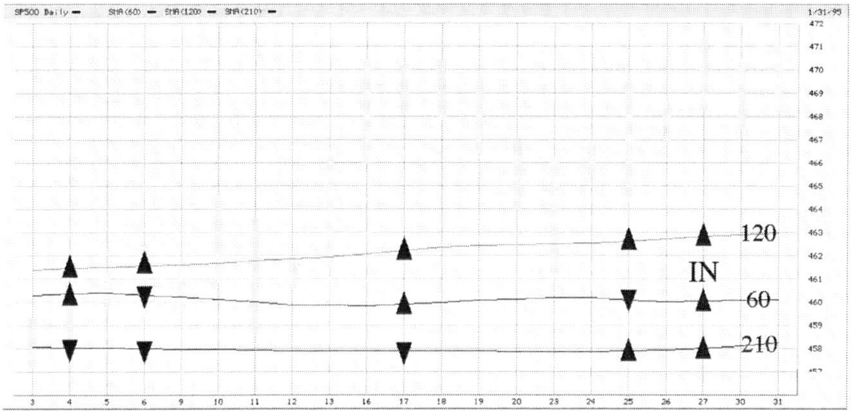

Figure 8-7: First "IN" signal for the S&P 500 Average, January 27, 1995. The arrowheads indicate the trends of the 3 moving averages (MAs), and are shown each time one of the 3 MA trends changes direction. The trends representing the 60-, 120- and 210-day moving averages all were trending upwards on this date, but not earlier. A new uptrend is not indicated until all 3 averages trend upward, as seen in the 30-day display.

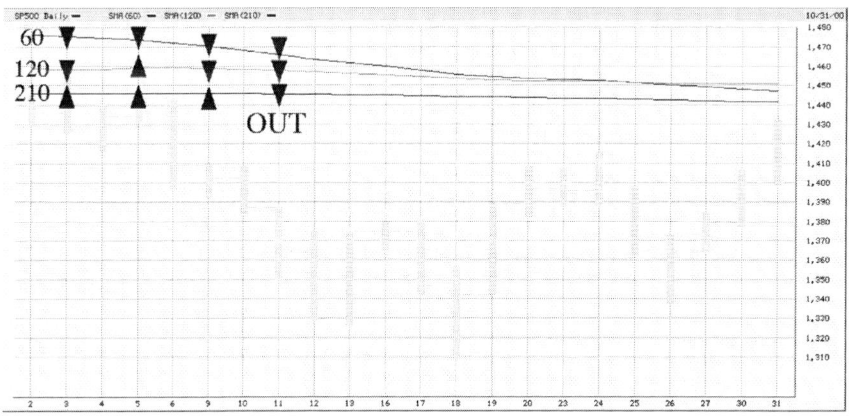

Figure 8-8: "OUT" signal for the S&P 500 Average: October 11, 2000. The arrowhead direction indicates either an uptrend or downtrend for one of the three MA trends. The lines representing the 60-, 120- and 210-day moving averages all were trending downwards on October 11, reversing the "IN" signal of January 1995, and a bull market which had lasted over 5 years.

Figure 8-9: S&P 500 Average from 2002 to 2009, with 60- (▲), 120- (■) and 210- (●) day moving averages providing "IN" and "OUT" signals on May 14, 2003, and December 17, 2007 respectively.

Applying exactly the same methodology to the S&P 500 Average over the next 7 years, from 2002 to 2009, an "IN" signal was generated in May 2003, followed by an "OUT" signal in December 2007 (Figure 8-9). The techniques thus allowed participation in a second long-term bull market with a market exit at an appropriate time. The overall results of application of the market monitoring system from the beginning of 1995 to the end of 2009 is summarized in Table 8-1.

In the plot of January 1995 (Figure 8-7), the three signals do not all trend upward, as is noted, until January 27, when a signal to buy index funds tracking the S&P 500 was indicated. In October 2000, all three averages show a negative slope, or trend, on October 11 (Figure 8-6). The 210-day moving average, having the longest period, changes the most slowly, and tends generally to reverse trend least.

The System allowed one to participate in the bull markets extending from 1995 to 2000 and from early 2003 until late 2007 while avoiding

S&P 500 Average: 1995–2009

	Using: The System					Buy/Hold
Date	**Signal**	**Index**	**Profit/Loss**	**Time**	**$10,000 Growth**	**$10,000 Growth**
1/3/95	Initial Index	459.10			$10,000	$10,000
1/27/95	In	470.40				
10/11/00	Out	1364.60	$19,009	5 yrs, 9 mos	$29,009	
5/14/03	In	939.30				
12/17/07	Out	1445.90	$15,646	4 yrs, 7 mos	$44,655	
12/31/08	Final Index	903.30				$19,680

Summary of Results:

With the System:
Change in capital: +444.6%
Mean rate of return: +11.2%
$10,000 becomes $44,460 in 14 years
# of trades = 4 in 14 years
Long-term gains > 1 year: 2
Short-term gains < 1 year: 0

With buy-and-hold strategy:
Change in capital: +96.8%
Mean rate of return: +5.0%
$10,000 becomes $19,680 in 14 years

Table 8-1: Summary of results of using buy-and-hold strategy and the monitoring "System" for mutual funds based on the S&P 500 Average from 1995 to 2009. The growth in a $10,000 investment over the period for "System" and Buy-and-hold strategies are summarized in the 2 columns at the right. The average annual rate of return for the "System" is more than twice that of buy-and-hold.

two major downtrends. The upmarket participation was for periods of at least four years, allowing the indicated capital gains to be taxable at the much lower long-term (greater than one year) rates. The mean annual capital rate of return, ignoring dividends and trading costs, was more than double than that achieved with a buy-and-hold approach.

We might note that only longer-term trends have been called by the System in this analysis, as we wanted. This is a consequence of using the rather long periods represented by the three moving averages, and requiring a unanimous decision for trading decisions.

So far, so good. The monitoring system developed for use in U.S. markets, as represented by funds tracking the S&P 500 Average, has performed very well compared to a buy-and-hold strategy for the period of years we have chosen to study. In the next chapter, I will discuss the application of this monitoring approach to funds tracking important international stock indices.

CHAPTER 9

EXTENSION OF THE SYSTEM TO INTERNATIONAL MARKETS

In the last chapter, a successful system for trading index funds based on the S&P 500 Average was described. In order to achieve useful diversification, it seems worthwhile to see whether the monitoring system developed for the S&P 500 Index can be extended to other markets. There are of course a large number of stock market indices and index funds that track their movements.

An International Approach

One reasonable approach is to invest in the largest and most developed world economies, to achieve more participation in the major markets of an increasingly globalized world. To achieve this, one can invest in stock index funds tracking the markets of the European community and Japan. The European Union GDP approximates that of the United States, with a total in 2008 of $18.9 trillion U.S.[1] The markets of the largest European economies are components of the MCSI (Morgan Chase Securities International) Europe Index. The total GDP of the countries in the MSCI Europe Index is very close to U.S. total GDP in 2008 of $14.3 trillion U.S.[2] The MSCI Europe Index is tracked by index funds such as the Vanguard European Index Fund (symbol: VEURX).

The second largest single national economy after the United States is the market of Japan, with an estimated 2008 GDP of $4.8 trillion U.S.[3] The Japanese market indices are followed by relatively few index funds in the United States, one being the iShares Japan Index Fund (symbol: EWJ), which tracks the MCSI Japan Index. By selecting these three funds (S&P 500 Index Fund, VEURX, and EWJ), one will be participating in the economies of the three largest world economies, whose aggregate GDP represents well over half that of the global economy.

When one invests internationally in this manner, one is not only increasing stock diversification among a much larger number of individual stocks, but is also simultaneously achieving currency diversification, since the individual stock prices and resulting indices reflect not only the average stock price levels, but also the relative value of the currency of denomination. This effectively represents a hedge against drops in the relative value of the U.S. dollar, which may turn out to be a worthwhile feature of such index funds in the future.

The VEURX Fund (Vanguard European Index Fund) qualifies as a low-fee fund with a MER of .4. There is currently a 1% "short-term trading" fee for shares that are held for fewer than 60 days, and that could theoretically be somewhat of a problem if one's trading system indicates a sale fewer than 60 days after a purchase. While this may indeed happen at some point, it would hardly represent a major blow; in context, market indices such as those tracked by VEURX often go up or down more than 1% in a single day. The iShares Japan Index Fund (EWJ), as noted

Figure 9-1: Vanguard European Index Fund (VEURX) plotted from 1995 to 2002, with 60- (▲), 120- (■) and 210- (●) day moving averages providing "IN" and "OUT" signals on March 20, 1995, and September 6, 2000, respectively.

Figure 9-2: Vanguard European Index Fund (VEURX) plotted from 2002 to 2009, with 60- (▲), 120- (■) and 210- (●) day moving averages providing "IN" and "OUT signals on May 21, 2003, and January 17, 2008, respectively.

previously, is an ETF. It also qualifies as a relatively low-fee fund with a MER of .52%.

It is possible to analyze the price movements of the VEURX fund using exactly the same approach used with the S&P 500 Average. The graphs (Figures 9-1 and 9-2) and the summary (Table 9-1) show the results of extending the market monitoring system described in Chapter 8 to this fund from 1995 to 2009.

Why We Need to Use 3 MAs

Again, I would stress that while these graphs are useful illustrations of the price movements and trading signals involved, all trading signals were generated using the one-month displays on BigCharts. The use of three simultaneous moving averages is often seen as beneficial compared to a simpler technique over various periods, particularly in times of indecisive or "sideways" markets. In 1999, for example, European markets trended sideways for an extended period (see sidebar). Since the markets eventually continued a prior uptrend, it was best to continue to stay in the market over this period. If one inspects the courses of the three moving averages over early 1999 in, their combined effect in reducing unnecessary trading is evident. The system indicates that one should have stayed invested in European stocks for two long bull markets from 1995 to 2000, and 2003 to 2008, while avoiding the bulk of the serious declines in the intervening years.

Real markets tend to have such sideways periods every once in awhile. *Requiring a unanimous judgment of multiple averages frequently tends to minimize signals that would lead to excessive trading.* Although the approach sometimes fails, failures are relatively few. In the application of the monitoring system to the iShares Japan Index Fund (Figures 9-4 and 9-5), there were a couple of "failures" of the system, leading to rather rapid switching in and out of this fund.

How Costly Is a "Failure" of the System?

It is probably a good idea to consider just how painful it will be for us if an unnecessary and unprofitable signal is given by our system and we act on it. If we are dealing with a large fund company such as Vanguard or Fidelity, and trade out of their S&P 500 Index Fund into a bond fund or money market fund, and then back into the S&P 500 Fund again, there will generally be no effect of transaction costs on our bottom line, since such funds do not charge for such exchanges within their own fund families. If one switches in and out of the Vanguard European Index Fund, there is a 1% charge (penalty) for fund positions held fewer than 60 days. If one switches in and out of an ETF such as iShares Japan, relatively small transaction costs of a small fraction of 1% would be paid for the trades in and out of the fund. When one considers that stock market indices very often move more than 1 percentage point per day, the transaction cost penalties are certainly tolerable.

We certainly want to minimize our trading for the important reasons of overall simplicity and tax considerations, but we won't suffer too greatly from the occasional bad call that is inevitable for any technical system. Our goal cannot be technical trading perfection; the important thing is to recognize and stay with the long-term trends.

Table 9-1 summarizes the results of using the monitoring system initially developed for the S&P 500 Average (the System) applied to the Vanguard European Index Fund for the period from 1995 to 2009. This

SIDEWAYS PERIODS IN STOCK MARKET INDICES: WHAT YOU SHOULD KNOW

If one doubts the necessity of using multiple, rather than a single, moving average to track markets, the not-infrequent periods of sideways market movement should provide rather compelling support for the concept of using more than one MA as an indicator. In all markets we will be considering, directionless periods of market movements have created difficulty in discerning the general market trend, and have the potential to generate excessive and unprofitable market signals. An example of such a period, and of the utility of using multiple MAs simultaneously, can be seen in European markets throughout all of 1999 (Figure 9-3), a particularly indecisive year for these markets. In the plot below, the five-month period from February to June 1999 is shown for the overall European market in the form of the plot for the VEURX Fund and the 60-, 120-, and 210-day MAs.

The position indicated by our system at the start of 1999 was "IN" the market. It is instructive to consider using the criteria for all three MAs to agree on an "OUT" signal, compared to the indications that would have been provided by any individual signal. At time point A in February, only the 60-day MA uptrend keeps us in the market, and at time point B, only the 120-day MA was in a uptrend, again keeping us in the market. At point C, the uptrend in the 60-day MA keeps us in the market, and the uptrend in the 210-day MA in June at D again keeps us in the stock market. The three-MA system keeps us in the market for the entire year of 1999; the market then trended more sharply upward until the "OUT" signal of September 2000.

Relying on any one MA as a signal would have resulted in several unnecessary and unprofitable trades, and may have severely tested our faith in our ability to monitor such markets at all using a technical system.

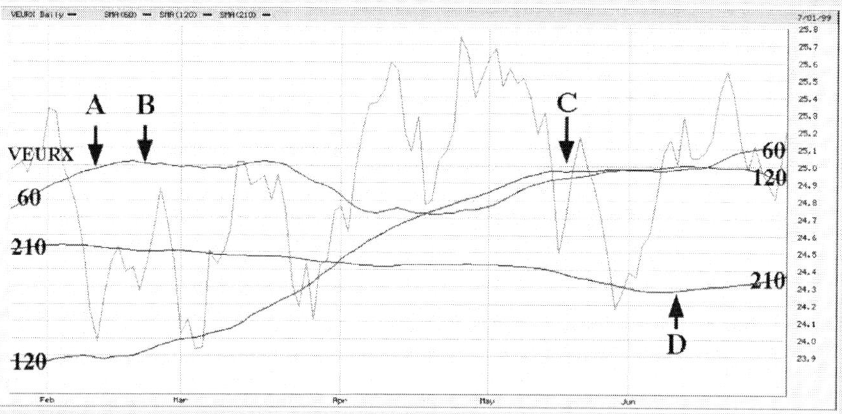

Figure 9-3: A five month period in 1999 demonstrating the necessity for using three moving averages.

table again compares the use of the System to a buy-and-hold strategy for an initial investment of $10,000.

The performance of the monitoring system is somewhat better than that achieved for the S&P Average over the same period. The pattern of market index movement over this period is very similar to that of the S&P, although these markets have not tracked as closely in the past. In any case, the advantage of using the monitoring system compared to a buy-and-hold strategy was an increase in rate of return of 7.7% per year on the average. As for the S&P, a total of four trades allowed for two rather lengthy periods in the market in which capital gains would have been taxed at long-term rates.

Vanguard European Index Fund (VEURX): 1995–2009

	Using: The System					Buy/Hold
Date	**Signal**	**Index**	**Profit/Loss**	**Time**	**$10,000 Growth**	**$10,000 Growth**
1/3/95	Initial Index	11.71			$10,000	$10,000
3/20/95	In	12.15				
9/6/00	Out	27.30	$12,469	5 yrs, 6 mos	$22,469	
5/21/03	In	17.16				
1/17/08	Out	36.02	$24,695	4 yrs, 8 mos	$47,164	
12/31/08	Final Index	20.41				$17,430

Summary of Results:

With the System:
Change in capital: +471.6%
Mean annual change: +11.7%
$10,000 becomes $47,160 in 14 years
# of trades = 4 in 14 years
Long-term gains > 1 year: 2
Short-term gains < 1 year: 0

With buy-and-hold strategy:
Change in capital: +74.3%
Mean annual change: +4.0%
$10,000 becomes $17,430 in 14 years

Table 9-1: Summary comparing of buy-and-hold strategy to the monitoring system for the Vanguard European Index Fund (VEURX) from 1995 through 2009. The growth in a $10,000 investment over the period for "System" and Buy-and-hold strategies are summarized in the 2 columns at the right. The mean annual rate of return is almost three times that for buy-and-hold.

Extension to the Japanese Stock Market

The iShares Japan Index Fund (EWJ) has been in existence for a relatively short time, and data is only available for analysis since 1997. Figures 9-4 and 9- 5 provide a graphical summary of the monitoring system applied to this fund. The results of applying the monetary system to the ishares Japanese Index Fund (EWJ) from 1997 to 2009 are summarized in Table 9-2.

As we can see, the results were not as simple as the applications to the S&P 500 Index and VEURX. There were a total of ten trades over twelve years, with three long-term gains, and two short-term losses. Relatively small losses were incurred for trades made during rather lengthy sideways markets in 2004/05 and 2006/07.

The two trades resulting in losses in 2005 and 2007 illustrate the problem of "failures" of the monitoring system, and some indication of the losses that can result. It is inevitable, in fact, that such failures of any

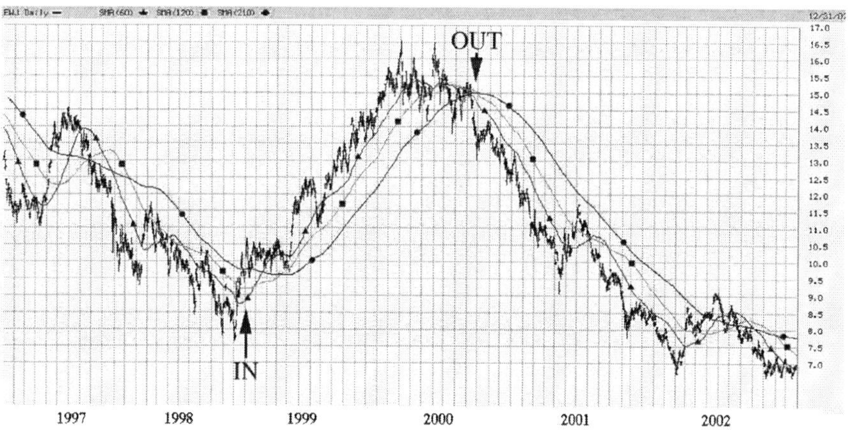

Figure 9-4: iShares Japanese Index fund (EWJ) plotted from 1997 to 2003, with 60- (▲), 120- (■) and 210- (●) day moving averages providing "IN" and "OUT" signals on November 2, 1998, and July 24, 2000, respectively.

Figure 9-5: iShares Japanese Index fund (EWJ) plotted from EWJ plotted from 1995 to 2002, with 60- (▲), 120- (■) and 210- (●) day moving averages providing "IN" signals on 7/3/03, 5/5/05, 8/10/05 and 12/4/06. "OUT" signals are given on 7/24/00, 4/28/05, 5/12/05, 11/8/06, and 8/28/07.

computer-based monitoring system over time will occur, resulting in unnecessary and unprofitable trades. Recalling the Zweig/Davis system discussed in Chapter 10, it may be noted that about half of trades made with this particular monitoring approach resulted in relatively small losses compared to the gains.

The best we can hope for is minimization of the number and magnitude of losses created by such failures. The number of extra trades in EWJ might be considered as four, since both an extra exit and return to the market resulted on two separate occasions. The two bad calls resulted in a loss of about 2.5% of the committed capital each time.

The extra trades would not have proved very costly, using a discount broker, compared to the substantial improvement over a buy-and-hold strategy over the 12-year period.

iShares Japan Index Fund (EWJ): 1997-2009						
	Using: The System					Buy/Hold
Date	Signal	Index	Profit/Loss	Time	$10,000 Growth	$10,000 Growth
1/2/97	Initial Value	13.06			$10,000	$10,000
11/2/98	In	10.44				
7/24/00	Out	13.75	$3,170	1 yr, 8 mos	$13,170	
7/3/03	In	7.75				
4/28/05	Out	10.07	$3,943	1 yr, 10 mos	$17,113	
5/5/05	In	10.45				
5/12/05	Out	10.16	–$475	7 days	$16,638	
8/10/05	In	10.68				
11/8/06	Out	13.63	$4,596	1 yr, 3 mos	$21,234	
12/4/06	In	13.99				
8/28/07	Out	13.7	–$440	10 mos	$20,794	
12/22/08	Final Value	9.58				$7,330

Summary of Results:

With the System:
Change in capital: +107.9%
Mean annual change: +6.3%
$10,000 becomes $20,794 in 12 years
# of trades = 10 in 12 years
Long-term gains > 1 year: 3
Short-term gains < 1 year: 0

With buy-and-hold strategy:
Change in capital: –26.7%
Mean annual change: –3.1%
$10,000 becomes $7,330 in 12 years

Table 9-2: Summary of buy-and-hold strategy compared to the monitoring system for 12 years from 1997 to 2009. The growth in a $10,000 investment over the period for "System" and Buy-and-hold strategies are summarized in the 2 columns at the right. A respectable rate of return of 6.3% was attained using market monitoring, while the buy-and-hold strategy produced a negative rate of return over the study period.

A Perfect Monitoring System Is Not an Option

It may be that the discouragement created by failures resulting in losing trades could lead to one's discontinuing the use of such a system of monitoring. Unfortunately, perfection in the performance of a market index monitoring system is not an option; such systems will always result in some losses. Ultimately, we can only design and stick with the best system we can come up with based on the historic record of market index movements. Otherwise, we really have no option but to return to the buy-and-hold strategy, which has not worked very well for quite some time.

The overall rate of return of 6.3% per year for EWJ from 1997 to 2009 was lower than for the U.S. and European markets, but the 9.4% advantage over a buy-and-hold strategy (a 6.3% gain compared to a –3.1% loss with buy-and-hold) was the greatest of any market at which we have looked.

I believe enough evidence has been presented to show that the market monitoring system suggested to you has potential to enhance your returns when investing in funds that track the most important indices of the major world economies. By investing in just the three types of funds I suggest (S&P 500 Index, European, and Japan Index funds), you would be participating in an extremely well-diversified group of major stocks. Likely 90% of the great world stocks we can name are represented in the markets in which you would be participating, and the monitoring system can clearly give us a substantial edge in performance. I will be summarizing my ideas for an overall system of investment in Chapter 13, but this is basically the approach I believe we should be using with the portion of our funds allocated to the stock market.

CHAPTER 10

USEFULNESS AND LIMITATIONS

The last two chapters have described techniques for trading stock funds based on the major world stock market indices. It has been shown that the methods used have been capable of substantially improved rates of return over the last 14 years, compared to a buy-and-hold strategy. It seems important to address the questions of just why such methods might be effective, and what the limitations on their use might be.

Why Does the Monitoring System Seem to Work Well (or at all?)

A natural question is why the proposed market monitoring system seems to work when many prior efforts at market monitoring are generally felt to have been unsuccessful? It would seem the answer lies in both in the monitoring approach that is used and the type of data to which it has been applied.

Looking first at techniques to time markets, in Chapter 7, reference was made to a variety of fundamental technical and graphical techniques that have been used to time markets. By "fundamental" I mean the general predictions of the course of markets from newsletter writers and market professionals based on their best efforts to integrate available economic and market data to arrive at a judgment. The stock market, on the other hand, represents the ultimate financial democracy, and its level and movements over time encode the collective judgment of all participants. History tells us that while isolated judgments by individuals may occasionally be correct, market movements related to the larger collective judgment cannot be consistently predicted by any one person, based only on their individual view[1]. The inconsistency and sporadic nature of market predictions of this type hardly recommends the approach for a serious, organized approach to market monitoring.

Technical analysis approaches have the benefits of potentially removing the human factor, and looking instead for patterns of prior market movements useful in detecting market trends. Such analysis can be repeated as frequently as needed, rather than relying on intermittent pronouncements. These advantages give technical analysis the possibility of useful long-term application in a systematic way[2].

We have discussed general technical analysis tools, such as the Wall $treet Week (W$W) technical index, and the put/call ratio formerly presented in the *New York Times*. There is little historical justification for the utility of such techniques, and as discussed in Chapter 7, these tools seemed capable only of analyzing general stock market sentiment, which is of limited practical value. Graphical techniques based on pattern recognition, while having achieved some success in monitoring in the past, often rely on rather subjective interpretation of market patterns. Neither approach seems ideal for an organized, continuing quest to monitor major market trends.

The Zweig/Davis approach to trend analysis for market monitoring[3] and the approach I have proposed use computer-generated measures, which can be repeated every day as often as required to provide unambiguous indications as to the market's likely trend. Such a methodology has characteristics affording a realistic, systematic approach to market monitoring. Similarly, in the previous chapter, a technique for using three moving averages of major stock market indices as the basis for deciding whether to hold stock index mutual funds was described. The system seems to be effective likely for the reasons described above; the time periods over which market changes occur is unpredictable, and relying on a unanimous verdict for three relevant periods seems capable of providing a useful tool for determining your current position. The numerous oscillations of different periods about the major trend may be sampled effectively with the three averages, and requiring unanimity of all three for a trend reversal limits excessive trades.

It should be stressed that the monitoring system is designed to look only for long-term trends in stock market indices. The longest moving average of 210 days corresponds to almost 10 months, and a reversal of a market trend extending over this period is necessary for the overall system to indicate a change of market course. Day-to-day and even week-to-week stock market movements and the explanations for these proffered in the media should be considered as noise, and not concern us. While the media are required to comment (basically) on the recent daily or weekly market trends, or the last couple of months of market movements, we will do best by ignoring these variations.

The constant composition of low-volatility stocks making up these indices is also very important, since significant alteration of composition can be expected to change characteristics of index movements over time, and we are trying to identify future trends based on past movements. The major world indices analyzed have two characteristics, then, that make them likely candidates for analysis for trend-following techniques: relatively low volatility about trend lines, and constant composition of component stocks. It is fortunate that these major market indices have such desirable characteristics, since our goal has been to find a method of stock investing based on their corresponding stock index mutual funds.

Limitations of the Monitoring System

From the above discussion, it would appear unlikely that actively managed funds, for which this monitoring system was not designed, would be good candidates for our monitoring system. Actively managed funds tend to have high turnover rates, averaging 85% per year for U.S. stock funds[4]. If one attempts to employ a monitoring algorithm to the movements of such funds, the constantly changing character of the fund mix of stocks ensures that one will be making measures of a changing entity, and it becomes unlikely that past movements will provide reliable indication of future trends.

While the stocks represented by the S&P average represent about three-fourths of U.S. stock market capitalization, the point is often made that they are not the whole market[5]. As discussed in Chapter 4, the stock market is often divided up into categories based on market capitalization and "style" as value, growth, or a blend of both. The market capitalization ("market cap") of a stock is the total cash value of all its shares. Small caps may be defined as those with capitalization of less than $1 billion, mid caps $1 billion to $5 billion, and large caps more than $5 billion.

The styles are imprecisely defined; growth stocks have higher earning growth potential, and value stocks have lower valuation and lower growth potential. It has been found in a number of studies that the performance of these different categories are often somewhat different when viewed over various time periods[6].

Historically, U.S. small capitalization stocks have generally outperformed the larger ones, so it might be desirable to diversify beyond the large cap stocks of the S&P 500. A common index of U.S. smaller stocks, which is tracked by a number of mutual funds, is the Russell 2000 Index, and these may represent suitable vehicles for participation in U.S. small stocks.

The problem as I see it, though, is that the volatility of small stocks is so great, unlike the relatively sedate price action of the large cap stocks I have discussed so far, that even indices averaging a great many of such stocks are too volatile—too noisy to analyze in the manner I have suggested in the last two chapters.

The parameter *Beta* is a descriptor of both the market volatility of individual stocks, and how closely a stock tracks the S&P 500 Average. Values of Beta are normalized to 1 for the S&P 500 stocks, but the average Beta for the Russell 2000 stocks is about twice as high. Figure 10-1 below is a plot of the S&P 500 Average from 1995 to 2009, compared to the Russell 2000 Index.

There are a few relevant observations concerning Figure 10-1: the basic patterns of bull and bear markets are similar, especially in the last six years, but the Russell 2000 Average data is quite a bit noisier. When one is performing a market-based monitoring technique such as that which I have advocated, noise is not your friend since it makes monitoring more difficult. Moving averages have been used in the system I propose to smooth out and reduce the temporal noise in the index data, but the very noisy nature of the small cap index data makes it less suitable for the sort of analysis I advocate. If one would like to participate in small cap stocks in U.S. markets, a reasonable approach might be to invest in an index fund mirroring the Russell 2000 Index, but to trade on the basis of signals generated by the movement of the stabler S&P 500 Average. Another relevant observation, perhaps the most relevant, is that if you look closely at the plots above, *the historic performance advantage of small stocks has not been evident in recent years.*

There are, of course, a great many indices available around the world beyond those of its three largest economies, and it would seem desirable to participate in the future growth of emerging economies in Asia and South America, for instance, over the coming years. The price action in stocks and even market indices of these emerging economies is much more volatile than those of the developed world, however. While it may in the future be possible to adapt the approach we have used to these markets, the monitoring system as described earlier cannot be expected to work well in these markets without modification.

Since the three markets studied represent well over half of world GDP[7], the ability to gain an edge in these important markets gives System practitioners a realistic chance to outperform markets long term. It seems prudent to restrict our monitoring to these indices, and their corresponding index mutual funds described in Chapters 8 and 9, at least for the present.

Figure 10-1: Comparative plots of the Russell 2000 and S&P 500 Average from 1995 to 2009. The Russell 200 Index shows more volatility, but the overall gain over the period is about the same for the two averages.

Source: BigCharts

CHAPTER 11

SOME EXPECTED CRITICISMS AND PROBLEMS

I've shown the results that can be obtained in U.S. and international markets with the system for stock market monitoring I've developed, and that I suggest you use as part of an organized approach to stock investing (the System). I've thought about the responses of stock market professionals and individual investors, and have tried to foresee the likely response to my discussions of the System and its performance.

Firstly, from investment professionals, what I primarily expect is a good deal of skepticism. Although it is hard to predict all criticisms, I'll list some of the major probable objections and my responses to these below.

1. *The proof submitted is all retrospective. Many systems have been developed that seemed to work well in the past only to fail in the future. Past results are no guarantee of future performance.*

I've put this criticism first, since it is the most obvious criticism, and it has some validity. In introducing my system, I indicated that the change in market character that seemed evident in the 1990s in U.S. markets caused me to restrict my analysis to the years since then. It is very possible indeed that the character of these markets may change again, and render the methodology I have been using less worthwhile or completely useless.

In my discussion of the likely future of U.S. markets in Chapter 14, I will discuss why I think a change in market character is unlikely for some years—perhaps eight or ten years, in fact. This reasoning is based on historical data on U.S. markets that I will detail, which tend to show bull periods of about 17 years alternating with bear-to-sideways markets of the same length, such as the one we are in right now[1]. The last major U.S. bull period clearly ended in 2000, and we likely have quite a few years left in which a buy-and-hold strategy will continue to underperform the approach I advocate.

The only market type, in fact, in which a buy-and-hold strategy will really work well is a sustained bull market over many years, such as that seen from 1982 to 2000. Many of us are still remembering these wonderful years for investing, and tend to think of it as a normal period, when it is actually unusual historically, and seems the least likely type of market for some years to come.

Some may say that it would have been nice if I had written this book a couple of years ago, before the major downturns in world markets in 2008. The monitoring system's sell signals in all world markets near the end of 2007 were quite convincing, in fact, all coming so close together. It seemed clear that it was time to retreat to the fixed-income world. The importance of avoiding such future severe downtrends has actually been an impetus to my writing this book, and hopefully the methods I have outlined will be useful to you in avoiding the bulk of future declines, while capitalizing on uptrends. Since the meltdown in world markets in 2008, it seems more important than ever to try to build back portfolios, and hopefully the advantage afforded by the monitoring system in the past will persist and provide assistance in the future.

Data from the past is all we currently have available to analyze. To state the obvious, it is not possible to create and employ in the future a market monitoring approach based on analysis of any data other than past data, since this is the only data currently available. The historical basis for my recommendations on market monitoring are not very different from that leading to any specific recommendation concerning future investment strategies. As discussed in Chapter 4, a number of authors recommend investing in stock index funds rather than actively managed funds, and this appears very good advice based on analysis of the available data on fund performance. We might note, however, that these astute recommendations on the virtues of index fund investment are all based on data from the past; *no future data is available for analysis at the present time.*

The best I can do regarding the future is to suggest that I may write another edition of this book in five or ten years, and will be able to follow up on the previous success of the monitoring techniques I have evaluated thus far. As noted previously (Chapter 7), Martin Zweig did a ten-year follow-up in the second edition of his book *Winning on Wall Street* of his technical system for stock market trading. Very similar performance was seen over the follow-up compared to the initial period of years evaluated[2], and marked continued superiority was demonstrated for his approach compared to a buy-and-hold strategy.

2. *Systems using moving averages are nothing new. These have been used for decades and nobody has ever come up with a system based on them that has been useful in market monitoring.*

I wouldn't be very impressed with this argument, but it could be raised. While it is certainly true that moving averages in general are old hat, there are compelling reasons to exploit them in a system of trading such as I have outlined, based on my initial criteria for a desirable system.

My goal as stated at the beginning of the chapter is to develop a practical, simple technique for identifying major longer-term price trends in major stock indices on which low-cost index funds are based. I believe the system I have presented fulfils the criteria I initially outlined, since it is rather easily implemented using freely available online analysis tools, and has given very good results over many years compared to a buy-and-hold strategy. While there has been considerable general discussion of the possibility of using moving averages over various periods of time to discern short- and longer-term market movements, I haven't seen anything like this very effective system for recognizing long- term trends in major markets, presented previously.

It is noted in chapter 10 the unchanging mix of low volatility stocks in major stock indices provide the perfect situation for such trend analysis techniques.

3. *There is no accounting for the costs of transactions and the loss of dividend income when not in the market.*

The system was designed to recognize major trends and avoid excessive trading. No trend-following technique is perfect, and there have been unnecessary trades and there will be more in the future. Trading is only indicated about once every two years using the proposed system, and the costs of such trading are minimal. If one has an account with a major U.S. fund company such as Fidelity or Vanguard, there will generally be no fees, or minimal fees for shifting from an index fund to a bond fund, or vice versa. Since one will be primarily in bond funds when not in stock index funds, and the interest distributions are typically a couple of percentage points higher than stock dividend distributions, there should be no significant loss in revenue. The fees for purchases and redemptions of ETFs such as the iShares Japan Index Fund are very low, when performed through an online discount broker. I don't think these costs are significant problems.

Some Straw Man Arguments

There are some other criticisms of market monitoring that are in the nature of straw man arguments. These, of course, are rhetorical devices in which one attributes to an opponent an obviously false or doubtful argument, just to knock it over or rebut it.

For example, I've seen the criticism that is something like, "It is not possible to get out at the top and get in at the bottom." When one is using a trend-following approach such as I suggest, however, one is basically guaranteeing that this will never occur; it takes time for the "in" or "out" signals to develop, generally well beyond the corresponding market top or bottom. If you check out the charts of the indices followed and the positions of the signals, you can readily see that the signals are generally at least 10% lower, sometimes much lower, than market tops and higher than market bottoms. The point is to avoid the bulk of the market drop and take advantage of most of a long-term bull run, not to get in at the top and out at the bottom.

You're Not Really Gambling If You Have a Winning System

No system of monitoring the stock market can expect perfection. The method I've described can give you the means to be successful most of the time, which should provide success over the long term. At the risk of extending my casino gambling analogy further than I should, I do consider the market monitoring approach not dissimilar to a winning strategy for blackjack. Blackjack is the one standard casino game that can actually be won by an individual with the requisite skill, and the winning strategy relies on counting "tens" (which are face cards and tens), as the game of blackjack proceeds. The "lower than tens" to "tens" ratio in the pack is initially 36/16, but if the ratio falls below 1.65 (as can be determined by counting tens), the individual player becomes greatly favored[3]. There is a "tens-rich deck," and the player will usually win since the dealer will likely "bust," or go over 21. The individual player then should increase their bet to five times their original bet. Nevertheless, the dealer may still luck out and draw 21, winning the hand.

I think of the market monitoring approach in quite similar way. When a market configuration indicates the start of an uptrend, it is time to buy the corresponding index fund. Based on the clear historic record, you are much more likely than not to be taking advantage of a long-term trend. Occasionally the signal will not work, comparable to the dealer drawing a 21 in blackjack, but the odds are significantly in your favor. Even if one signal proves not to work, you don't change your system either in blackjack or the stock market, but continue to play the odds. Considered this way, a gambler or investor is hardly trying to predict; they are just playing the odds in an intelligent manner.

You also have an advantage over the gambler in that nobody can throw you out of the stock market when you're on a winning streak, but they are sure to throw you out of the casino (or worse) if they think you are counting tens.

Some Practical Objections

As to individual investors, I can see at least a couple of objections to their implementing the system I have proposed, and I am sympathetic to their concerns. I can sort of hear expected responses in my ears, and I'll try to suggest what individual investors' objections might be.

1. *I can't possibly look at the results of the stock markets' movements every day, and figure out what to do.*

Well, the good news is that you don't have to. This system is just concerned with very long-term fluctuations in market indices, and you only need actually to check on the recommendations it gives once in awhile. It is hard for those of us who get the news online or on TV to avoid the general trends of stock prices; when the market direction is not in doubt, there is no need to check on what the trading system recommends. In the 1995 to 2000 period on the S&P Average, the continuous uptrend was obvious, and there was little need to keep checking for a signal to exit. In the entire year of 2008, markets had been trending downward all year—you really didn't need to keep checking on the system's recommendations; it clearly continued to say "stay out!" The current market will have to stabilize for many months before you will need to check for a signal to get back into index funds.

2. *I really don't have the time to do this. I'm too busy.*

I can understand this objection; I'm busy too. I have defined a monitoring system for market index funds as simple as I could make it and explained it as clearly as I can. The time spent to set up and occasionally check on the indications will be well worth the effort, particularly for an individual with substantial capital at stake.

A System Index Fund Incorporating Market Monitoring?

I have tried to be practical and realistic in my assessments thus far, and I must admit that it may not be realistic for some investors to follow the methods of market monitoring I suggest. The methods require a bit of computer skill; even more important, they require a degree of interest in investing and discipline in following the selected market data. They also require the confidence not to equivocate, but to go ahead and make the trade when the signal is flashed.

It has not escaped my attention that an obvious way to exploit the monitoring system for market index funds (the System) and allow for public participation without the necessity of individual market monitoring would be to create a mutual fund that might integrate the monitoring function in its program of investment. Such a fund would allow the advantages of the market monitoring system to be used, in conjunction with index mutual funds and bond funds, while not requiring continual input from individual investors. Since setting up and managing low-cost index funds requires considerable expertise and capital, the hypothetical fund could be a "fund of funds," participating in markets through index funds run by major financial companies. Such a fund could fully exploit the monitoring tools, refining them and extending them to other market indices over time. Perhaps such mutual funds will be available in the future.

CHAPTER 12

RISK MANAGEMENT

The most successful investors know that limitation of the downside risk is really important. Warren Buffet has said that the first two rules of investing are: Rule #1: Don't lose your money; Rule#2: Never forget rule #1. Two basic approaches to avoiding substantial losses are summarized below.

Diversification

The necessity of not having all one's eggs in one basket is a bedrock investment principle, similar in importance to the concept that risk and return on investment are generally highly correlated. While there are a number of subcategories of risk, we should be concerned with the possibility of a significant loss in a single stock or bond. This type of risk is dealt with quite effectively by our plan of only investing via stock index funds and bond funds that typically are compilations of hundreds of individual issues. The damage from default or significant drop in price of any one stock or bond is of negligible importance.

We have further considered the possibility of extending our stock holding among a number of categories of U.S. stocks (Chapters 4 and 10) and bond funds of various risk levels, in order further to guard against relative underperformance or capital loss in any particular category.

While this standard sort of diversification is fairly straightforward using the fund approach, we also should likely be considering some other important types of risk, including inflation/interest rate risk, and currency risk in making up our portfolio of mutual funds.

We considered currency risk briefly in Chapter 9, in which the use of foreign stock index funds was discussed. The basic concept, of course, is if your money is all in funds denominated in U.S. dollars, and the dollar goes down in value compared to other currencies, the value of your U.S.-denominated assets will take a hit when seen in global terms. I'm quite a believer in participating in the developed world economy using this approach, while simultaneously hedging currency risk. Typical advice is to have 15% or so of total assets in foreign markets, but 30% might be more effective in attaining real diversification into foreign markets.

As discussed in Chapter 4, the risk of inflation increasing, with an accompanying increase in interest rates, is an important consideration. Since such jumps in inflation tend to be unpredictable, purchasing bond funds with average maturities no longer than five or six years is prudent, since interest rates will go up, and longer-term bond prices will drop significantly if inflation becomes a serious problem.

Further forms of diversification beyond the scope of this book would be required to hedge against an eventual resurgence of inflation, which seems a realistic possibility. Stocks would be likely to perform poorly, as they did in the late 1970s and early 1980s, and long-term bonds would likely suffer serious losses. One may have to look beyond stocks and bonds to real estate, collectibles, commodities, and precious metals for shelter in such a storm.

Market Monitoring as a Risk Management Technique

While diversification is the classical tool for risk management in investing, if one has some confidence in their ability to switch between asset categories using market monitoring techniques, an additional tool for risk management becomes evident. The sort of switching to which I am referring is from stock index funds into bond funds or money market funds when "out" signals are generated in a particular market.

If one feels that they have the ability to time stock index funds with some effectiveness, and since the rate of return on the stock component tends to be higher (though much more volatile), it makes sense that one might consider investing a higher percentage than the standard allocation in stocks, if market monitoring is used. Since the system I am recommending includes switching completely out of stock index funds when "out" signals are given, one will not be exposed to the bulk of the decline, and greater returns can be made from the stock component via the higher-percentage allocation.

No strategy is risk-free, of course. It is possible, for example, that a horrendous (and as yet satisfactorily explained) one-day price drop, such as the 22.6% drop on the Dow on Black Monday (October 19, 1987) could happen again, and catch us flat-footed[1]. This sudden cataclysmic drop, however—by far the largest one day drop in the history of U.S.

markets—would likely have proved quite devastating irrespective of one's investing approach.

Still, if market monitoring works reasonably well, it should be considered a risk management tool. Consider the bar graphs of performance in Figure 12-1 below, which is a summary of various U.S. stock fund categories for the year 2008.

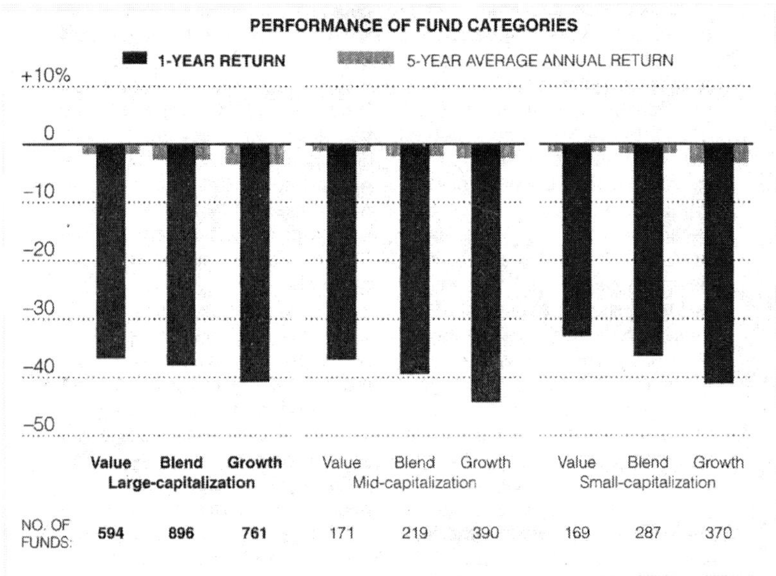

Figure 12-1: Bar graph of the one- and five-year annual returns for various categories of U.S. stocks at the end of 2008. The performance of the various options for investment is very similar, and there would have been little benefit from diversifying among these.

Source: The *New York Times*, Business Section, January 1, 2008.

Inspection of the plot indicates that, while 2008 was not a typical year, being one in which all asset categories declined significantly, there was little benefit from diversifying among major classes of U.S. stocks. A much more effective risk management approach than having allocations among many of the different categories represented above would have been using the monitoring system for U.S. markets I recommend, which would have kept one completely out of all these markets in 2008.

There is actually a bit of a trade-off here regarding the asset allocation approach to diversification and the use of market monitoring. In order to have finely tuned asset allocation among various stock categories, it might be necessary to hold quite a large number of individual funds. Unfortunately, one becomes less and less likely to actually pull the trigger and make the trades indicated by a market monitoring system when one has a complex portfolio designed carefully to balance among asset categories.

CHAPTER 13

THE SYSTEM: PUTTING IT ALL TOGETHER

In earlier chapters, I discussed appropriate vehicles for stock and bond investment. Regarding stock market investments, the conclusion was reached that the best way to invest is via U.S. and foreign stock index mutual funds. The advantages of excellent diversification, very low transaction and management fees, and minimization of taxes flowing to the investor make these funds the clear choice. In the fixed-income area, in addition to a small component of money market funds, short-to-intermediate bond funds and bond index funds make the most sense, with low fees being even more critical here.

A system for market monitoring of stock index funds was also presented that has allowed in the past substantial advantages over a buy-and-hold strategy. The advantage in return rate over buy-and-hold for the monitoring system applied to U.S. and foreign stock index funds has ranged from 6.2% to 9.4% per year in the last 12 to 14 years.

In this chapter, I'll talk about integrating the ideas presented so far into a system that should lead to superior investment results over the long term, and yet hopefully retain the virtues of simplicity. Simplicity has been a major goal, but it is sometimes necessary to incorporate features that might add complexity.

As discussed earlier, a buy-and-hold strategy based on low-fee index funds is a proved one that is very simple to implement. We would like to improve performance beyond that approach if we can.

It is difficult to see how the fixed-income portion of our portfolio can outperform the overall bond market, since the only approach imaginable would involve the ability to predict the future course of interest rates, and whether a huge flight from risk as in 2008 might occur in the future. I can see no way to predict such factors. The stock portion of our portfolio is the part in which to look for enhanced performance above the mean, and there are two approaches that might work: improved performance by active management of stock selection, or market monitoring. We have already noted that while the former possibility sounds logical and attractive, it has quite consistently failed whenever it has been fairly tested. This leaves only stock index market monitoring as a possible tool for enhanced performance beyond buy-and-hold.

To be useful, a market monitoring system must be realistically usable by the average person, capable of providing unambiguous indication of whether to be invested in stocks, and enable you to access the results of the system on a daily basis if desired. In addition to these desirable mechanistic features, it should also be proved capable of actually providing a significant advantage in improving investment results over time.

I believe the monitoring system outlined in this book has these virtues, and that combined with a straightforward integration of monitoring into the management of a portfolio based on stock index funds and bond funds, it forms a sound basis for investing both taxable and tax-deferred retirement accounts. Such an integrated system should prove a powerful investment tool, and I have named it "the System" to stress the systematic integration of a number of concepts (market monitoring, index funds, low fees) into an organized, winning strategy.

A System for Asset Allocation

There are quite a few factors affecting your ability to apply the System to your personal investing. Different considerations apply to different types of investment accounts, and there are a number of different types of investment vehicles to be considered. For a system to be practical, it has follow the overriding principle of simplicity or it will not be practical for an average investor.

Taxable vs. Tax-Deferred Accounts

While the principles of investment are the same for both regular and tax-sheltered accounts, the financial instruments available for the two situations may be somewhat different. Unlike the choices you make in setting up your personal taxable accounts and IRA accounts, the 401(k)-type funds of every company or organization are set up by the enterprise in somewhat different manners, and the investment vehicles available differ widely. There is not even any requirement that these plans have a stock index fund as an option, so it will likely be necessary to modify your approach depending on the availability through your individual plan. In the steps below, I'll indicate some possible alternatives in 401(k) plans, dependent on just what options you have available.

Stocks vs. Bonds

The first step is deciding on the percentage allocation to stocks (in the form of stock index funds) and fixed-income investments (in the form of bond funds). As discussed earlier, as one grows older and approaches retirement, the mix suggested often is to select a fixed-income percentage corresponding to the investor's age. The concept here is that as one approaches retirement, and will soon be requiring the proceeds of retirement savings to finance the retirement years, the allocation to relatively risky stocks should gradually be reduced to minimize the possibility of significant capital loss. This is an effort to fine-tune risk management in the critical time period approaching and beyond the start of retirement.

As to the primary allocation of funds committed to the U.S. stock market, by far the best idea is to use a low-fee index fund for the S&P 500 Average, such as those of Fidelity and Vanguard for the bulk of this, even for all of your U.S. stock allocation. As previously noted, the S&P 500 does not represent the entire U.S. market, but it does represent about 75% of the total U.S. stock market capitalization. In order to achieve some better balance into small stocks, you might put perhaps one-quarter of your U.S. stock allocation into a fund tracking the Russell 2000 Index, or any diverse or "blend" small U.S. stock fund.

You will likely be partially invested in fixed-income securities (bonds) at all times, and more fully, or wholly, when the time has come to exit particular stock index funds. Bond funds and bond index funds holding short to intermediate debt having maturities no more than five or six years are a good compromise between interest-paid and interest rate-risk. As discussed in Chapter 4, it is not a good idea to chase a bit more yield by going out further in maturity, since a resurgence of inflation and interest rates can cause severe drops in the prices of long-term securities. As to the category of debt, I favor having the majority in investment-grade short-to-intermediate-term corporate bond funds.

Money Markets

While an allocation of a specific percentage in a money market fund is generally recommended for emergencies, I'm not sure this is really necessary, since if one has primarily short-term debt in bond funds, one can readily sell shares in such a fund and have the proceeds in a couple of days. While money market funds do have the advantage of always having contributions available at par, the interest provided is generally a couple of percentage points below that of a good investment-grade short-term bond fund, so minimization of funds in money markets seems a good idea.

U.S. vs. Foreign Markets

As to allocation within the stock market fund index category, while generally an allocation of about 15% of an investment portfolio is given as a maximum allocation to non-U.S. stock index funds, a larger allocation to foreign index markets—perhaps 30%—might be advised, largely for diversification among markets, and to hedge substantially against currency risk. In recent years, there has been quite a strong correlation between the U.S. and the European and Japanese markets, and it has been useful to follow the major indices of all three as a sort of check on whether global markets are confirming signals on any one index.

Minimizing the Number of Funds

Asset allocation schemes are often presented that are much more complex than the scheme suggested above. My approach is in general to keep things as simple as possible; it is important to minimize the number of funds one is using if one is going to complement their funds-based strategy with a market monitoring system. From personal experience, I can tell you that if you are planning to trade based on market monitoring, your fund structure has to be as simple as possible, or when the time comes to change your position, you will likely hesitate, since it may seem too complex to trade a relatively large number of funds into other funds. There should be no reason to participate in more than three or four stock funds. *I keep my fund allocation simple, and typically have no more than a half-dozen total funds at any one time.*

Integration of the Monitoring System

The use of the monitoring system presented in Chapters 8 through 11 is quite straightforward. I have simply set up the monitoring system for the three major U.S. and international index funds I have been using (Fidelity or Vanguard S&P 500 Index Fund, Vanguard European Index Fund, and iShares Japan Index Fund). As indicated in Chapter 10, since the higher volatility of low-cap U.S. stocks and the low-cap indices is likely to make the indices themselves poor candidates for direct analysis in the trading system, the simplest approach is just to follow the S&P 500 Average, and use signals based on this average to trade all U.S. stocks. In other words, if the S&P 500 Average signal says to get out, one should exit all U.S. markets, since these have historically been highly correlated.

As stated above, the vehicles available within 401(k) plans are highly variable, which creates difficulties in applying the monitoring system. Virtually all 401(k) plans, however, have one or more options that contain, or are most heavily weighted to, U.S. stocks. These should be converted into the fixed-income options when an "out" signal on the S&P 500 Average is given, since all U.S. markets are quite strongly correlated. Hopefully your plan will have something resembling a short-to-intermediate high-grade bond fund. If not, a substantial allocation in a money market fund is worth considering when it is time to stay out of the market.

When the monitoring system gives the signal to get out of stocks, or to get back in, you have to act rather decisively. You just need to look at the record of past performance (Chapters 8 and 9) to see that this is true. When one exits stock funds, the proceeds from these can just be transferred to bond or bond index funds, or possibly to money market funds. The whole integrated system has been built around this concept of trading when the monitoring system dictates.

I have presented the simplest system of market investing that I have been able to devise, and one that seems capable of superior performance over the long term. I feel that the system I suggest is appropriate for long-term use by individuals. It should be possible to perform the steps suggested without much difficulty or the requirement of inordinate amounts of time and attention.

CHAPTER 14

THE FUTURE

Any predictions as to the future course of the economy and markets over a period of years are fraught with difficulty, and such prognostications should be regarded with considerable skepticism. On the other hand, it would be very useful for us to have some idea of the more likely economic and market scenarios confronting us over the coming years in order to plan our general investment strategy. If we felt that the conditions of 1982 were going to be present sometime soon, for example, we might want to abandon any thoughts of market monitoring strategies, since in 1982 the U.S. stock market was poised for an unprecedented 18-year romp upward, increasing 10 times in value.

Prognostications from the Past: How Helpful Are They?

Over the years my experience has been that the course of the economy, inflation, and stock markets have more often than not proceeded in unexpected directions, rather than in those generally predicted by economists and others. In 1982, after a long period of stagnant stock markets, few were predicting the beginning of a huge expansion; pessimism was the general order of the day following a long bear market. More recently, in early 2008, I don't recall hearing or reading of an impending global financial crisis. There was considerable discussion at the time among the sages as to whether a recession could be avoided, when we had actually been in one for months.

If one reads the news and financial journals at any time, including the present, one can find a great deal of evidence and advice that would appear to support any and all possibilities for the likely future market direction. The lesson to take away is that the various predictions that are offered every day in the print media are as likely to be wrong as right. While we can understand that newsletters and business columns in newspapers feel they must offer some assessment of the likely future course of markets, we will be best off if we ignore them.

While it is probably best to disregard all such predictions, perhaps we can learn something from an historical look at stock trends in the United States over fairly long periods of time. The whole approach to the system of investment I have proposed is based on analysis of historical price movements. If we look at the U.S. stock market over the past century (Figure 14-1), we can get an idea about the broad price movements over periods of decades and perhaps learn something useful.

Learning from Market History

The *Wall Street Journal*[1] published just such a retrospective look at U.S. markets in late 2008, and noted that market movements may be divided into major bull and bear markets, as indicated in Figure 14-1 below. Notice that there have been rather lengthy periods, generally about 15 to 17 years long, of stock stagnation despite substantial price swings. Alternating with these have been long bull markets, the most recent being from 1982 to 2000. In broad historical terms, we appear to be in a major bear period now, beginning in 2000.

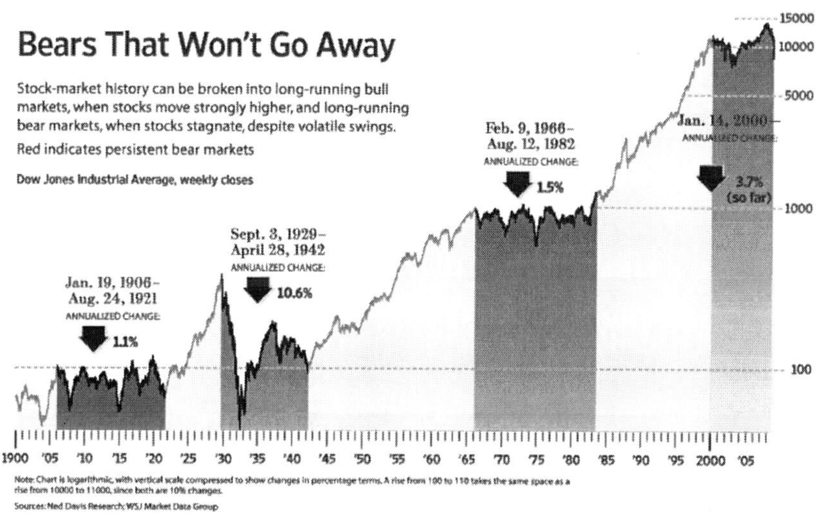

Figure 14-1: Logarithmic plot of the Dow Jones Industrial Average from 1900 to the present showing major bull and bear markets indicated by shading. The lengths of bear markets have averaged about 16 years.

Source: Zweig, J. What History Tells Us About the Market. *Wall Street Journal*. October 11, 2008.

At the time of writing in early 2009, scarcely a week went by when I didn't see an article by one or more well-known experts noting that the best time to buy is when markets have gone down a lot, and fear rules, such as at the present time. While it certainly would be better to be a buyer now than a year ago, it is difficult to know whether decreased price levels at this point really provide a reason to purchase stocks. Where is the bottom?

Perhaps we should note the opinions of Robert Shiller, Professor of Finance at Yale University and chief economist for MacroMarkets in his book *Irrational Exuberance.* He has likely the most impressive record of predicting market directions of any individual I have read. In 2000 Dr. Shiller forecast the crash of the NASDAQ market, and in the second edition of his 2005 book, he described the striking overvaluation of residential real estate[2]. In the *Wall Street Journal* article referenced, Dr. Shiller's techniques of market valuation are discussed; evaluation of the historical valuation of U.S. stock markets with comparison to current valuation would clearly seem a rational approach to determining the likely future market direction. He plots a 10-year moving average of the price/earnings (PE) ratio on major U.S. stocks adapted from that of the legendary investor Benjamin Graham[3]. What tends to happen to stock valuations in long bear markets is just the opposite of bull markets; they tend to become lower and lower as investors become progressively discouraged.

In the summer of 1982, after a 16-year bear market, the most recent in U.S. history, the Graham PE (moving average of the PE ratio over ten years) was 6.6. In October 2008, the Graham PE stood at about 15, compared to an historical average of 16.3, as compiled by Dr. Shiller. The major implication of this seems to be that stocks are not really very undervalued by historical norms in spite of the huge price drops in 2008. An important factor to consider, of course, is that earnings in U.S. corporations are declining quite swiftly, and the prognosis for corporate profits in the future is not necessarily good.

In a somewhat similar manner, the *New York Times* has detailed the evidence that, even with the high stock prices of October 2008, stock prices were still not cheap by historical standards[4]. In Figure 14-2—the inflation-adjusted U.S. stock market average (S&P 500)—the mean stock earnings/share adjusted for inflation and the Graham PE since 1937 provide a window through which to view current stock valuation levels.

As we can see, the Graham PE is only slightly below its long-term average, and earnings are indeed falling (and likely to fall substantially more). The general trend of valuation as expressed in the Graham PE, shown in the rightward graph, shows that near the end of long-running bull

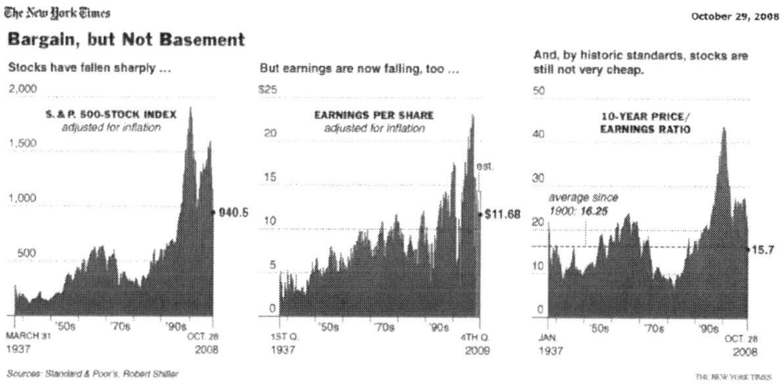

Figure 14-2: Measures of stock market valuation since 1937: inflation adjusted market average, mean stock price/earnings per share, and the "Graham PE."

Source: Leonhardt, D. Are Stocks the Bargain You Think? *New York Times*. October 29, 2008.

markets, there has tended to be an expansion of valuation as expressed in this parameter. In the year 2000, for example, the Graham PE reached a record of over 40. At the end of the 1981–1982 recession, the value was under 7. There would certainly appear to be plenty of future room for significant decreases in corporate earnings and reductions in overall stock valuations, which are the rule in recessionary periods. The market does not really look undervalued at present, based on the historical record.

Dr. Shiller, as noted in the *Wall Street Journal* article, is wisely quite averse to making anything resembling a firm prediction of future movements in the price of U.S. stocks. However, it was noted that, for a Graham PE similar to the 1982 low, the S&P 500 Average would have to decline to about 400, and the Dow would fall to approximately 4,000. These levels would imply about a 50% drop from current prices. Since the current major market bear trend appears to have begun in 2000, we are likely only about 8 years into the current broad stock market trend, which is about half the expected historical length of a bear period in U.S. markets. Also, from the discussion above, it looks as if U.S. markets likely have a way to go before valuations reach those typically seen at the end of bear markets. From these considerations, it seems we may expect that U.S. markets will likely continue their sideways to downward trend for quite a number of years. We can reach this conclusion both on the basis of the average length of bear cycles in the past, and the fact that stock prices do not appear undervalued in historic terms.

The Problem with Debt

Looking at the larger economic picture in the United States, there is a single factor that looms very large indeed: debt. The current economic problems in the United States began with very high levels of mortgage debt for overpriced real estate, but personal debt via credit cards is also at very high levels. While national debt was decreasing around the year 2000, it has picked up substantially in recent years, and the huge costs of government borrowing for extraordinary economic measures are expected to bring annual fiscal deficits to well over $1 trillion. Recently, the *Economist* ran an article describing the growth of total debt in the United States, and presented a graph (Figure 14-3) summarizing U.S. total debt (all personal debt plus national debt)[5].

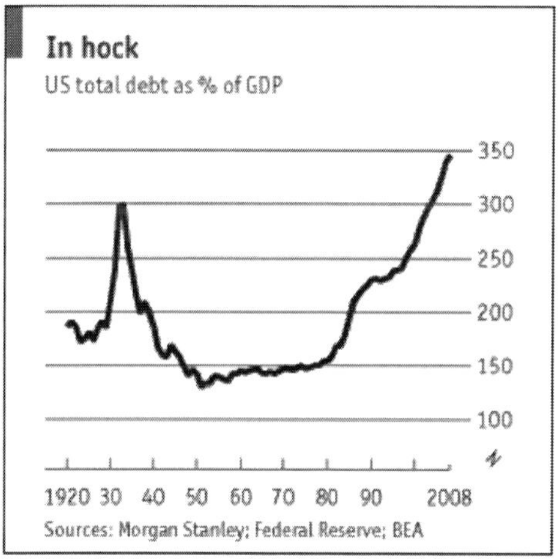

Figure 14-3: Plot of U.S. total debt growth since 1915. Total personal debt and national debt are summed and plotted over the indicated time period as a percentage of GDP. The current overall level of total debt in the United States is unprecedented.

The major problem with debt, of course, is that it has to be paid back eventually. It may be instructive to consider debt levels in earlier, less economically uncertain times such as the early stages of the Great Bull Market in the early 1980s. With debt at reasonable levels in relation to GDP, the country didn't have the huge debt overhang we now see, and the basis for a long period of expansion and rising stock markets was present. Unfortunately, total U.S. debt expanded rapidly along with rising markets and even after. Consumers in the United States saved about 9% of their disposable incomes from 1950 to 1985, but savings rates have progressively dropped to close to zero in early 2008[6].

Just about the only scenario available now is decreasing consumption in the United States, where consumer spending accounts for about 70% of the United States, and almost 20% of the world economy. Declining consumption will likely stunt economic growth, probably for a good time to come. It took over 20 years to build U.S. debt to its present level, and there is no reason to think that it won't take quite some time to address this problem; the implication of the plot above is that we will be likely be paying down the debt for a great many years. Also, it should not escape your attention that the only period comparable to the present in terms of U.S. total debt was the period around 1930.

The Likely Implications for the Future of Stock Markets

Historical considerations are most consistent with the continuation of a volatile but largely trendless to downward market for years to come. Unprecedented overall debt in the United States will likely continue to act as a brake on the economy. There is a significant likelihood that we are in another extended bear period that may well last for another 8 to 10 years. The average length of a bear period has been about 16 years, and we would only be about halfway along in the current substantial downturn. The most likely scenario for these coming years is that markets will exhibit discernible uptrends and downturns, but remain relatively directionless over the longer term, as they have for the past decade or so. The overall situation of 1982, with very low stock valuations and U.S. debt levels compared to the present day, is not on the near-term horizon.

Since a long-term bull trend seems unlikely for some time, a market monitoring strategy will likely be essential to attain superior returns in the future. Rather than simply purchasing stocks in the present environment in the hope of eventual gains over a period of many years, one will likely do better using a system based on past market movements, and one that has been successful in indicating when to participate in stock markets and when to retreat to fixed income.

CHAPTER 15

EVIDENCE-BASED INVESTING

I've tried throughout this book to highlight studies and techniques that have really proved capable of maximizing personal investment profits in past decades. For the components of the investing system I advocate, including the use of stock index funds and market monitoring, I have provided what I consider strong documentation—strong evidence of utility. In any field of endeavor, it seems intuitive to rely in the future on those techniques shown by the evidence to work well in the past. Such methods have been proved to have real utility, and they are what are often called evidence-based techniques today.

Evidence-Based Medicine

In contemporary U.S. medicine, the concept of "evidence-based medicine" is ascendant. This eminently reasonable approach is based on rigorous comparison of treatment techniques for certain disease processes, followed by medical practice in which only those treatments proved the most useful and cost-effective are employed to treat that specific disease. As health care reform is debated in the United States, there is considerable expectation that this approach will be essential to maximize the effectiveness of medical treatments while containing costs. It only makes sense to pay for treatments that have been proved the most beneficial, at reasonable cost.

While it's hard to fault a strategy directed by evidence of past effectiveness, it is distressing to note that the determination of the best treatment strategy for a given medical condition is very frequently not adequately defined. Even for a very common disease such as prostate cancer, there are very few studies effectively comparing the true utility of the various treatment options available, which include surgery, radiation therapy, and simple disease monitoring ("watchful waiting"). The major reason for the lack of definitive indications is the great difficulty of performing such studies well, since large numbers of patients must be treated with competing techniques, and treatment must be carefully followed for a great many years. It is often very hard or impossible truly to practice evidence-based medicine when the evidence of efficacy is unclear.

Although the implementation of evidence-based medicine is difficult, the logic behind such an approach is the best we can hope for. The most likely determinant of the best approach to future medical intervention is careful, rigorous comparison and analysis of the approaches that have been used in the past, and selection for use of those that have worked best. The desirability of this approach seems as clear for personal investing as for medical treatment. We can expect a certain randomness in the observed effectiveness of both medical treatments and investment techniques over time, but the smart money will always ride on those techniques that have proved most effective in the past. It is actually hard to imagine any other suitable approach.

Evidence-Based Investing

Fortunately, in the world of personal investing, the evidence indicating the most effective techniques for personal investment in the past is relatively clear-cut. A major goal of this book, in fact, has been to summarize and present analysis of relevant data indicating the most effective approaches, as detailed in the best available objective studies. I'll summarize the major principles arising from the key information presented so far below, with a view to integrating these into an optimal and practical approach.

1. Superior investment performance over time necessitates substantial investment in stocks relative to bond and money market investments. The chart of the relative performance of stock market compared to fixed-income investment at the beginning of Chapter 4 illustrates clearly the superior performance of stocks in the twentieth century. Although stocks have performed relatively poorly over the past ten years, the most likely scenario by far is the eventual return of superior stock market performance.

2. Low-fee stock index mutual funds are the only rational tool for stock market investing. Virtually every objective study of active portfolio management has indicated that this technique has resulted in average to somewhat subpar performance compared to stock index fund investing. When the effects of high fees for

active management and the inferior tax treatment of actively managed funds are considered, only index fund investing makes sense. Much of the overwhelming evidence for this statement is summarized in Chapter 4. Chapter 4 also presented documentation that the reports of stock analysts can be considered as pointless as the process of active stock management.

3. Fee minimization is essential if we are to achieve a satisfactory rate of return. In Chapter 5, the damaging effects of high fee structures were detailed, and the substantial benefits of using low-fee index funds stressed.

4. Market monitoring techniques applied to low-fee stock index fund investment can enhance the nominal capital gains from 6.2% to 9.4% per year for major world stock markets, compared to a buy-and-hold strategy. Chapters 8 and 9 showed that practical online market monitoring applied to trading of S&P 500, European, and Japanese major market index funds have provided this increment over the past 14 years.

The Implications of the Evidence Presented for Several Investing Strategies

In the foreword to this book, I described a couple of investment strategies as the "old dogma" and the "new dogma" of personal investment: the old dogma I defined as the active management of a stock portfolio by a full-fee manager, and the new dogma I defined as the individual use of low-fee index mutual funds. A comparison of the results attainable historically with such approaches was presented in Chapter 4. A third strategic option might be the use of U.S. and international low-fee index funds with occasional trading dictated by market monitoring (the System). What are the implications of the evidence summarized above for these approaches?

Comparison of "Effective" Rates of Return for Buy-And-Hold of Index Funds Compared to "the System"

As described earlier, a realistic rate of return must reflect the effects of inflation, taxes, and fees. I've called such a rate the "effective" rate of return. Let us consider the effective rates of return for using a buy-and-hold strategy with low-fee index funds, compared to such an approach enhanced using market monitoring (the System). In performing this calculation, it seems appropriate to use actual results of the 14-year period of analysis described in Chapter 8, in which the results of using these two techniques to invest in mutual funds based on the S&P 500 Index were documented.

In performing the calculations below, as in Chapter 5, we'll again assume 3% annual inflation and a 25% marginal tax rate, and estimate an annual MER of .25% for the low- fee funds used.

As shown for the 14-year period from 1995 to 2009 analyzed in Chapter 8, the nominal capital rates of return for the buy-and-hold strategy and System strategy were 5.0% and 11.2%, respectively, for the S&P 500 Index. If one does the math for the buy-and-hold strategy over the 14-year period, accounting for taxes (–1.25%), inflation (–3%), and fees (–.25%), the effective capital rate of return on the S&P 500 works out to only .5% over this rather substantial time frame.

Using the market monitoring approach of the System, we have shown in Chapter 8 that a nominal capital rate of return of 11.2% per annum was achievable from 1995 to 2009 for the S&P 500. Applying the same assumptions for taxes, inflation, and fees as for the buy-and-hold strategy, we can calculate the effects of these variables to again arrive at an effective capital rate of return. Subtracting the effects of taxation (–2.8%), inflation (–3%), and fees (–.25%), we arrive at an effective capital rate of return of 5.15% for this strategy.

While stock dividends would have boosted both the rates of return on stock calculated above equally, the superiority of the market monitoring approach (the System) to index fund investing becomes even more obvious when capital rates of return are calculated in this more realistic manner. In spite of its widespread acceptance in many quarters as the only realistic stock investment strategy, the buy-and-hold approach to index fund investing has provided a very minimal effective rate of return for many years. The System approach, on the other hand, has been proved capable of enhancing effective rate of return to a very respectable level.

Two Barriers to the Use of Techniques Shown Most Effective by the Evidence

While I look on the System techniques advocated above as a fundamentally attractive and proved approach to personal investing, it is certainly not that of most investors today. It would likely be profitable for individual investors to exploit System approaches, but there are important obstacles that inhibit individuals investing their hard-earned funds. The obstacles include problems with the standard model of investment advisory services, and characteristics of the average investor.

Problems with Advice, Advisors, and the Custodial Account Model

Examination of the historical record of what really works in stock market investing indicates that the best approaches are quite well defined, as discussed above, and should not be difficult to follow in principle. It would appear, however, that the most optimal techniques are not frequently exploited by average investors. There would appear to be a number of reasons for this situation, including lack of interest and knowledge of the principles of investment, difficulty in getting good investment advice in an efficient manner, and the structure of many advisory accounts.

As I have indicated earlier, it is important for all investors to receive solid investing advice on a regular basis. We have seen typical examples of the problems faced by individual investors in Chapter 5, in which teachers in both Nebraska and West Virginia chose very risk-averse investment strategies that resulted in very poor investment returns in 401(k) plans over time. Other individuals, no doubt, may have chosen inappropriate, very high-risk strategies, and likely lost much of their original capital. With a bit of guidance, such investors would likely have done much better.

Although I have called the custodial account model of active investing by a manager/advisor the "old dogma," it is likely the model currently used by the majority of higher net worth individuals. The problem in this approach is the forced combination of one service that has the potential to be useful to any investor (good current advice on overall investing and financial strategy) with a high-fee, actively managed investment portfolio.

When one initiates a managed account with an advisor, one combines the realistic goal of regular interaction with and knowledgeable input from the advisor, with an investment model that represents a triumph of hope over the evidence rather richly detailed in this book. When the account is set up, one will typically be shown some model portfolios, and there will be some indication that the research and experience of the particular manager will be capable of providing superior returns, but no meaningful data will be provided supporting the prospect of superior rates of return. The most likely prospect for the portfolio developed is actually subpar effective return, as detailed above and in Chapters 4 and 5.

As stated early in this book, a guiding principle for personal investing should be simplicity; our results will always tend to suffer when unnecessary complexity is thrust upon us. In Chapter 5, I discussed some of the complexities in taxation and retirement programs coming from government; we don't have much option here except to attain a general understanding and deal with them as best we can. An important drawback to the custodial account, in addition to its likely destiny of undistinguished performance, is the lack of flexibility it will immediately confer on future investment choices. The complex portfolios set up not only typically underperform, but their complexity makes the market monitoring techniques I advocate impracticable. Embracing simplicity and avoiding unnecessary complexity should be a key investment principle, and the actively managed portfolio is much more likely to add incremental complexity than incremental performance.

The Search for a Market Guru to Solve All Your Investing Problems

In a recent *Wall Street Journal* edition, a thoughtful article by Stephen Greenspan, emeritus professor of educational psychology at the University of Connecticut, explains "why we keep falling for financial scams."[1]

The article was primarily concerned with the history of such scams, and the psychological basis for participation by individuals. He discusses why he invested money in the Rye fund, which was basically a "feeder" fund for the Bernie Madoff empire:

"In my own case, the decision to invest in the Rye fund reflected both my ignorance and my unwillingness to remedy that ignorance. To get around my lack of financial knowledge and my lazy cognitive style around finance, I had come up with the heuristic (or mental shorthand) of identifying more financially knowledgeable advisors and trusting in their judgment and recommendations."

It is quite surprising to hear from highly intelligent professionals of their lack of basic investment information, lack of interest in learning, and lack of confidence in charting the financial waters. This attitude among investors seems very common, and can be truly dangerous to one's future financial health. Many individuals would really rather not learn even basic information about financial matters, or do any work, but simply hand their funds over to the man (it's usually a man) with the magic touch.

To draw another parallel with medicine, it is sort of like putting yourself in the hands of a famous medical practitioner or surgeon to treat your particular ailment. We all really want to believe in the skill of our physicians, since our lives may be in their hands. In an analogous manner, many would like to simply delegate their financial health to a famous financial practitioner.

The problem is that the evidence shows there are apparently important differences between these two fields. Although there are many problems in the practice of medicine, if you can obtain treatment by a practitioner who is very experienced in treating patients with your condition, your outcome will very likely be superior. The more experienced medical practitioner clearly will have a great interest in your condition, and is much more likely to be current on recent advances than a generalist. Experience really is critical in achieving superior results in fields such as specialized surgery; there are many studies demonstrating improved outcomes for specialist surgeons who treat far more cases than a more general surgeon.

In investing though, the evidence does not show that experience really is very useful in improving results. In Chapter 4, many studies demonstrated the inability of very experienced professionals using the best available data to obtain superior investment results. The tepid results obtained by highly experienced pension fund managers using the best available data, for example, illustrates this problem well. If these individuals can't obtain superior results using their considerable experience, why should you think it worthwhile to put your faith in some market guru?

The obvious danger evident from the quotation above is that the attitude expressed is that of an individual at great risk to be taken advantage of by a fraudster such as Bernie Madoff. While this is a potential peril, the odds are that such an investor will likely end up choosing a legitimate full-fee money manager who will arrange a complex portfolio featuring relatively poor effective returns. The uninvolved investor is much more likely to face a future of investment mediocrity than one of outright fraud. Neither outcome, however, seems particularly desirable.

Taking Charge of Your Financial Future

Rather than putting your faith in a guru, it is important to make an effort to at least learn the basics, and to take on something resembling an active role in investment. As noted, in the modern era, you are to a large extent the designated manager of your investments and retirement funds. Ironically, very basic knowledge of investing, which would allow much better investment decisions, can be acquired with minimal effort. The continual delegation of investing efforts without our active involvement prevents real learning, which is an always an iterative process involving participation and learning from mistakes.

The required principles for success well beyond the norm are really quite simple, even reading the present small volume should provide a start. Confidence, in the end, comes from actually doing something. Take the basic principles of investment dictated by past investing history and have at least some role in applying them to your personal investing. You will not find this difficult, and the process will provide a feedback loop with increased confidence allowing increasingly effective and less stressful involvement in the future. Whether you invest largely on your own or primarily with an advisor, the more you know, the better off you will be. You can do this; in the modern world, personal investing is a necessary skill one can readily learn and apply.

So What Should I Do Right Now?

You may be in general agreement that the most sensible approach is to invest based on the historical evidence of what really works. As discussed above, returns have been maximized over the past (almost) 15 years by using the System featuring a limited number of low-fee stock index and bond funds with trading directed by a market monitoring system. If it seems reasonable to apply these techniques to a portion of one's portfolio, what should our approach be at the present time?

When this book was written in mid-2009, world markets had come well off their lows in the spring, but had not as yet given "in" signals in U.S. or the major foreign markets (Europe, Japan) we have considered. A major turnaround in world markets starting in March 2009 continued in an impressive manner for long enough to generate System "in" signals in the three major market index funds whose markets have been evaluated in Chapters 8 and 9. Within a two week period in August 2009, signals were given to purchase the iShares Japanese market index fund EWJ (August 6), funds based on the S&P 500 Average (August 11) and the Vanguard European Index Fund VEURX (August 17).

These "IN" signals were even more bunched in time than the three signals to get out of these markets seen extending from late August 2007 to January 2008 (Figure 15-1). No doubt the increasingly globalized world economy with interdependence of economies has led to increasingly

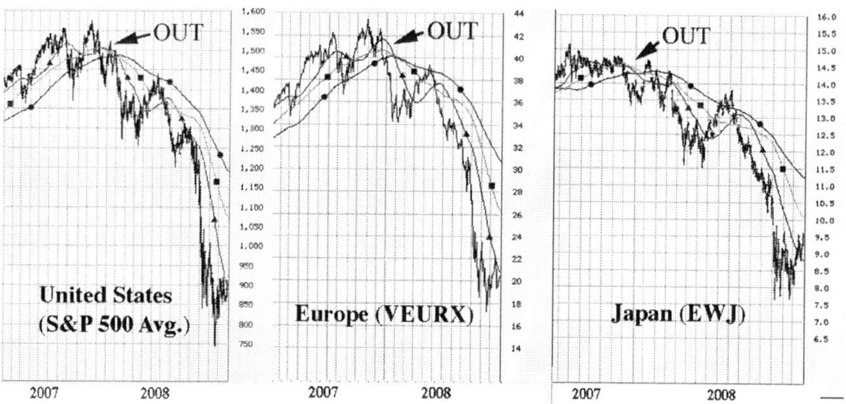

Figure 15-1: Plots of the US, European, and Japanese markets in 2007–2008, with "OUT" signals indicated on December 17, 2007, January 17, 2008, and August 20, 2007 for the US, European, and Japanese markets respectively. The "OUT" signals were determined using 3 MAs as described in Chapter 8. The correlation of price movement in the three markets is quite striking.

correlated world markets. In any case, the signals to get out of all world markets in late 2007 when all major markets flashed their "OUT" signals within months gave a prescient indication of the overall best course. It would seem a better than even bet that we have now seen a strong indication that the time to purchase index funds in these major markets has come once again.

It is very important, of course, that the fund selection is made so that no transaction costs (or at least minimal transaction costs) are incurred when future exchanges between fixed-income and stock funds are made. As in the discussion of these techniques in Chapter 13, the practical implementation of such a strategy differs somewhat for funds in 401(k)-type plans and taxable accounts. The great variability of 401(k) plan structures and the lack of requirement for inclusion of stock index funds will make it necessary to evaluate just what options are available in your particular case. Almost all such plans will have a fund heavily weighted to U.S. stocks, and this should be your investment fund of choice in this area. This makes sense since all U.S. stock markets are in fact highly correlated, and you will likely participate successfully in any future bull run. A similar approach can be taken to invest in an available European stock option (if available), using market monitoring of a fund tracking European markets such as the Vanguard European Index Fund (VEURX), or the iShares Japan Index Fund (EWJ).

For taxable accounts, funds can be placed in an S&P 500 Index Fund, or a foreign fund, in a manner similar to that suggested above for 401(k)-type accounts. There are generally no transaction costs charged for such switches between fixed-income and stock index funds of such large fund companies. If one chooses to participate in an ETF fund such as the iShares Japan Index Fund (EWJ), there will be transaction costs for buying and selling shares, which can be minimized using a discount broker.

It should be clear that having your funds in a handful of low-fee stock index and bond funds will provide substantial advantages over the old full-fee custodial account model. As discussed above, your effective rate of return will historically be significantly higher, and you will have the estimable advantage of simplicity as well. Rather than having your wealth dispersed in a great many issues and vehicles that you may not fully comprehend, you should be able to indeed wrap your mind around a portfolio of only a few stock index and bond funds. The continual and seemingly mysterious buying and selling in a custodial account will no longer be a distraction. You are very likely to have more peace of mind with an account that is comprehensible to you.

While the System's market monitoring approach has proved capable of greatly increasing stock market returns since 1995, a very important question is just how well is it likely to perform in the future? As noted in Chapter 8, there was quite a change evident in market dynamics around 1995, and it is possible that such a change could occur again, possibly rendering the market monitoring (System) approach ineffective. In Chapter 11 the point was made that in choosing to use market monitoring, one is basically playing the odds. If one believes that it is more likely that basic stock market patterns of the past decade and a half will continue in future years, one should use the market monitoring approach described. There really is only one other viable alternative: to adopt a buy-and-hold approach, hopefully featuring low-fee index funds. If you choose this latter strategy, you will be implicitly betting that market patterns are more likely to change in the future and render System market monitoring ineffective. Either way, you will be making a choice based on your individual perspective; it will be your decision, as it should be.

APPENDIX:

Key Background Material

In the 15 chapters presented thus far, I have tried to present a step-by-step discussion leading up to the description of a system, based on investment techniques proved to work best in the past, that I have used and recommend for personal investing. My purpose has not been to present a comprehensive reference on investing, nor to provide detail beyond what I felt was justified to support the approach I have taken in recent years.

In the context of what is now called the global financial crisis, a great deal has been written recently concerning the general economy and the behavior of stock markets. It has been a particularly interesting to be a reader of major financial journals and newspapers, and it has not been hard to find material highly relevant to my subject of personal investing. Below I reproduce with permission a number of recent articles from such newspapers as the *Wall Street Journal*, the *New York Times*, the *Financial Post*, and the *Economist*.

I have found a great many of the articles and other sources very relevant, and have reproduced some of the more compelling material below.

If you have found the discussion in this book to be of interest thus far, I am sure you will find this material of interest and value.

The order of the material roughly follows the sequence of information presented in the book. The first few items provide some illumination on the important question of investing for retirement. The first excerpt, from the remarkable *Four Pillars of Investing*, by William Bernstein, provides the results of a rigorous analysis of just how much we require to have saved prior to retirement. While this issue was mentioned in Chapter 3, the perhaps surprising results of such analysis, along with a description of some of the difficulties involved in retirement planning, are discussed much more fully here. The large sums of savings required for a decent retirement income and the effects of various uncontrollable factors are quite striking.

Will You Have Enough?

In *The Four Pillars of Investing*

William Bernstein

(McGraw-Hill, New York, 2002; pp. 229–234)

The Immortal Retiree

The best way to understand retirement saving is to work backwards. We'll spend the first half of this chapter attacking the problem of how much money you'll need on the day you retire, and the second half discussing how to get there. Along the way we'll find out that various market scenarios affect young savers and older retirees in radically different ways.

Let's start with what at first seems a silly assumption—that you'll live forever. This is an extremely easy thing to plan for, as long as you remember to think in "real" (inflation-adjusted) terms. And it's not that silly an assumption; in financial terms, retirement essentially is "forever." Among annuity and insurance purchasers—admittedly a healthier-than-average group—15% of surviving spouses, usually the wife, live to at least age 97. This means that many retirees will need to plan on more than 35 years of retirement. Financially, there's not much difference between living 35 years and living forever. To illustrate this, assume that all of your money is in a Roth IRA, meaning that you don't have to worry about taxes at any stage and that you'll need $40,000 per year in current spending power in retirement. If you earn a 4% real return, then you can withdraw that 4% of your nest egg each year without reducing your principal. You will be able to maintain this forever, since the nest egg's value will rise along with inflation. The 4% you withdraw from it each year for living expenses will also keep up with inflation. This means that you'll need $1 million (calculated by dividing $40,000 by 0.04).

Next, imagine earning the same 4% real return and dying on schedule after 35 years with *nothing* left over. In that case, since you will be spending down capital as well as earnings, you'll need only $746,585. (We'll discuss in a few paragraphs how this calculation is accomplished.) The key point is this—there's not a great deal of difference between living forever, which requires $1 million, and living for 35 years, which requires $746,585. Further, because of the uncertainties of the market and your own life, it's foolish to plan on dying on schedule with zero. This "back of the envelope" method of calculating retirement is a superb one—simply estimate your living expenses, including any taxes you'll owe on your retirement withdrawals, and adjust for what you expect from Social Security (which may not be much). Then divide by your expected real rate of return, as we did above. Four percent is a reasonable estimate, given the expected returns for stocks and bonds we calculated in Chapter 2. A more precise, but much more dangerous, technique uses the second example we described above—dying "on schedule" after 30 or 40 years with nothing. This method involves employing an amortization calculation, typically using a standard financial calculator, such as a Texas Instruments 11 BA-35, which can be bought for about $20. This is an extremely common procedure among financial planners and is computed in exactly the same way as a mortgage (except that in this instance you are the bank, receiving monthly payments until the "loan" of your nest egg is paid off). This is how we arrived at the $746,585 figure mentioned above.

To reiterate, amortization allows for no "margin of error." Make a few wrong assumptions, and you're eating Alpo in your golden years. How much margin of error do you need? Unfortunately, a lot. You see, all of the calculations we've done so far contain an extremely perilous *assumption—that our return is the same each and every year.* For example, in the calculation above we assumed that you'll receive a fixed 4% return that never changes, year after year. But in the real world, this does not happen. If you expect reasonable returns, then you have to bear risk. And by its very definition, the word "risk" means that you cannot expect to receive the same return each and every year. So you are going to have to live with the markets the way they are—good years and bad years, occurring in a completely unpredictable sequence.

The problem is that the precise sequence of the good and bad years is critical. This phenomenon was first brought to public attention by Philip Cooley, Carl M. Hubbard, and Daniel T. Walz of Trinity University. They looked at the success rate of various withdrawal strategies over numerous historical periods and came to the conclusion that only at a withdrawal rate of 4% to 5% of the initial portfolio value (i.e., $40,000-$50,000 of a $1,000,000 mixed stock-bond portfolio) do you have a reasonable expectation of "success." (Which they defined as dying without debt.) The scariest thing about their results was that the period they studied had real stock returns of 7%. Future stock returns are likely to be lower, which means that even their 4% to 5% withdrawal rate may be overly optimistic. On a more basic level, however, you can apply a much simpler acid test to your withdrawal strategy: What would happen if the day you retired at a market top, say on January 1, 1966, which marked the beginning of a long, brutal bear market, and you lived for another 30 years, until December 31 , 1995? For the first 17 years 1966–1982), the real return of the S&P 500 was zero. The return for the last 13 years (1983–1995) was spectacular, bringing the real return for the whole 30-year period from 1966 to 1995 up to 5.3%, not too far below the historical norm of 7%. To study this, I assumed that you began the period with $1,000,000 and then calculated results of various withdrawal rates from the following mixes: 1000/0 stock, 1000/0 bond, and 75/25, 50/50, and 25/75 stock bond mixes of both. I further assumed that the equity portfolio consisted of 80% S&P 500 and 20% U.S. Small stocks with five-year Treasuries as the bond component. The results of 7%, 6%, 5% and 4% withdrawal rates (that is, withdrawing $70,000, $60,000, $50,000 and $40,000 in real terms) are plotted in figures A(12)-1 through A(12)-2. Again, it is important to realize that the amounts on the vertical axis are in *inflation-adjusted* 1966 dollars.

These are profoundly disturbing results. Since real equity returns were 5.3% during the period, the conservative back-of-the-envelope method of withdrawing the real return every year should have allowed us to safely withdraw 5.3% annually and still have our real principal intact. In fact, such a withdrawal rate completely depleted all the portfolios, no matter what their stock bond composition. The amortization method predicts that we should have been able to withdraw 6.7% per year if we were willing to completely deplete the portfolio in 30 years. As you can see from

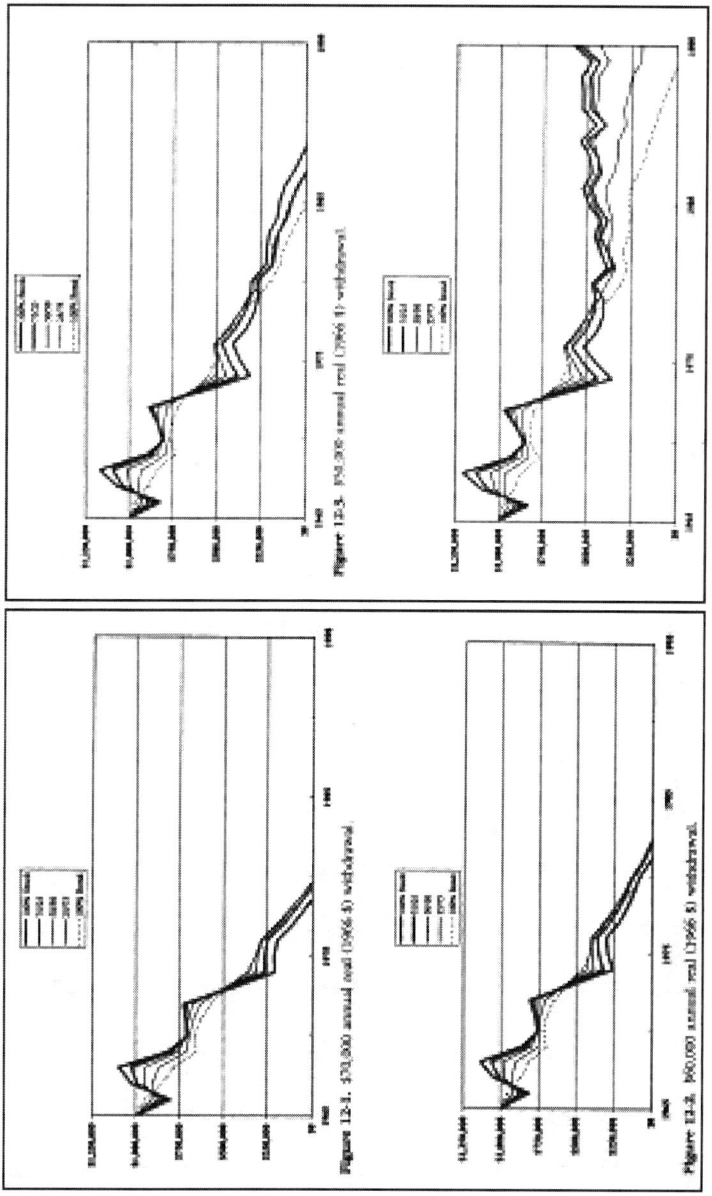

Figures A(12)-1 and A(12)-2: Rate of depletion of one million dollars over time for four different scenarios.

Figures A(12)-1 and A(12)-2, a 6.7% withdrawal rate would actually have depleted all the portfolios in about 15 years. This means that a "penalty" of about 1.50/0-2% was extracted by "the luck of the draw." In other words, a particularly bad returns sequence can reduce your safe withdrawal amount by as much as 2% below the long-term return of stocks. Recall from Chapter 2 that it's likely that future real stock returns will be in the 3.5% range, which means that current retirees may not be entirely safe withdrawing more than 2% of the real starting values of their portfolios per year!

It's important to understand that in all of the above cases, we have been talking about withdrawing a constant real amount of the beginning portfolio value. For example, in Figure 12-1, we withdrew a real $70,000—7% of a $1 million portfolio every year, increasing the initial $70,000 each year for inflation. This is *not* the same as spending 7% of the portfolio value each year. Were we to do that, we would withdraw less money each year as stock prices fell. For example, if stock prices immediately fell by 2006, we could only spend $56,000. Think about spending a quarter of your portfolio each year. You will never completely run out of money, although your portfolio value will vanish into insignificance after a decade or two. But if you can tolerate the fluctuations in withdrawal amounts inherent in a more reasonable constant-percentage withdrawal (say, 4% or 5% per year), then you will never completely run out of money.

RETIREMENT PLANNING

This fascinating, but possibly depressing, report by Hedrick Smith on the PBS program *Frontline* documents the inadequacy of the 401(k) process of retirement for many citizens. The entire 60-minute program (or at least portions of it), can be accessed using the URL below: (http://www.pbs.org/wgbh/pages/frontline/retirement)

The stories of a number of individuals are related, including several "retirees" who have not been able to retire, or who have gone back to work since their savings proved inadequate.

Can You Afford to Retire?

Hedrick Smith
Frontline
May 16, 2006
http://www.pbs.org/wgbh/pages/frontline/retirement

The baby boomer generation is headed for a shock as it hits retirement: many of them will be long on life expectancy but short on savings. The two main strategies for funding retirement—lifetime pensions and 401(k)-style savings plans—are in serious trouble. In "Can You Afford to Retire?" *Frontline* correspondent Hedrick Smith ("Is Wal-Mart Good for America?") investigates this looming financial crisis and the outlook for middle-class Americans.

"I think this is a crisis in the making," says Alicia Munnell, director of the Boston College Center for Retirement Research. "I think 10 or

15 years from now, people who approach their early 60s are simply not going to have enough money to retire on." "I would say, unless you're fortunate to be in the upper-income quartiles, that you're probably going to be in for a very rough ride," adds Jack VanDerhei of the Employee Benefit Research Institute (EBRI). "You're not going to have sufficient monies to pay the predictable expenses—your housing, your utilities, your food—plus the potential catastrophic medical care costs."

Half of America's private sector workforce has no employer-sponsored retirement plan; among the half that does, twice as many workers have contribution plans like 401(k)s than have lifetime pensions, a complete reversal from 25 years ago. The move from lifetime pensions to 401(k) plans has meant that employees now bear much more of the cost—and risk—for saving for retirement. According to the U.S. Department of Labor, in 1978 workers put in only 11% of total contributions to retirement plans, while corporations put in 89%; by 2000, the employee share had leaped to 51% and the company share had fallen to 49%.

A major driver behind this shift is a corporate bankruptcy strategy that enables companies to terminate lifetime pension plans through Chapter 11 bankruptcy. "Chapter 11 has become an effective tool for reorganizing a business," says Elizabeth Warren, a Harvard Law School professor and specialist in bankruptcy law. "It's like a knife on the surgeon's table. Bankruptcy is the official, federal, formal way to take legal promises and just slice them off." *Frontline* takes viewers inside the Chapter 11 bankruptcy of United Airlines. United dumped its pension plans, which were underfunded by nearly $10 billion, on the Pension Benefit Guaranty Corporation (PBGC), the federal agency insuring pensions that is running a $23 billion deficit. Because the PBGC only insures pensions up to a certain amount, many United employees and retirees saw their pensions slashed dramatically.

STOCK MARKET INVESTING: THE ADVANTAGES OF INDEXING

Yesterday's hearsay becomes today's mainstream. The concept of investing via low-fee stock index mutual funds has become widely accepted among those in the know today. While the major advantages of stock index mutual funds have been summarized previously, the "Motley Fools" give us their perspective on some important advantages of index funds in the online article to follow.

In spite of their rather unusual name, the Motley Fools are highly regarded for their investing insight. The superior performance of index funds based on the S&P 500 Index is described and the reasons for their marked superiority to actively managed funds detailed. The relatively strong performance of the stocks in the S&P 500 Average is a factor, but other factors including the much lower fee structure, lower turnover rate, and lack of perceived need for cash reserves all contribute substantially to index fund superiority.

"Investing in Index Funds"

The Motley Fool

http://www.fool.com/mutualfunds/indexfunds/indexfunds01.htm

Many stock investors turn to the letters Warren Buffett, CEO of Berkshire Hathaway (NYSE: BRK.A and B), writes every year to Berkshire's shareholders for some of the most valuable stock investing lessons available anywhere. But mutual fund investors have their own Buffet in John Bogle of the Vanguard Group, whose Common Sense on Mutual Funds contains a distillation of facts, figures, and analysis on mutual funds and are the most comprehensive and useful education that a mutual fund investor can acquire. Fools are certainly indebted to John Bogle, for showing clearly that—contrary to what you may have read on countless magazine covers—mutual fund investing is extremely simple: Buy an index fund.

(Psst. There's a reason that all these magazines don't tell you how simple mutual fund investing really is. Scientific marketing surveys and focus group testing have determined that magazines with covers that read "Index Funds: Still The Best Choice!!!" every single month really wouldn't sell as well as magazines that promise "Our BRAND NEW 10 Best Mutual Funds To Buy RIGHT NOW!" Sad, but true.)

In 1975, John Bogle presented an idea to the board of directors of the newly formed Vanguard Group—create an extremely low-cost mutual fund that would not attempt to beat the returns of the stock market as measured by Standard & Poor's 500 index instead, it would attempt to mirror the index as closely as it could by buying each of the index's 500 stocks in amounts equal to the weightings within the index itself. In his presentation to the Vanguard board, Bogle presented the historical data then available to him. In his account of The First Index Fund, Bogle writes:

> *"I projected the costs of managing an index fund to be 0.3% per year in operating expenses and 0.2% per year in transaction costs. Since fund annual costs at that time appeared to be about 2.0%, I concluded that an index fund should reasonably be expected to provide an annual return of +1.5% above a managed fund."*

In the intervening years Bogle has proven to be even more correct about indexing than he had predicted he might be. Since then, the gap between the performance of the market and the performance of actively managed mutual funds taken as a whole has actually been significantly wider than the 1.5% theorized by Bogle in 1976. During the 1990s, the total shortfall between actively managed mutual funds and the market as measured by the S&P 500 has so far been a whopping 3.4% per year.

The differential between actively managed funds and passively managed index funds is very easily explicable. The difference does not come from the actively managed mutual funds being run by buffoons. Not at all. The stocks that mutual fund managers pick end up being more or less average performing stocks. Bogle analyzes the differential as being determined by four factors: costs, turnover, sector, and cash reserves.

During the 1990s, the S&P 500 has provided an annualized return of 17.3%, compared with just 13.9% for the average diversified mutual fund. This 3.4% is explained first by understanding the fact that during the 1990s the S&P 500 (essentially an index of the 500 largest companies in America) has produced returns that are better than the rest of the market. One must first look at an index of the whole stock market, the Wilshire 5000 Index. The return for the Wilshire 5000 has been 16.3%

during the 1990s, so you should count 1.0 percentage points as a "large-cap effect," bringing the gap between managed funds and the Wilshire 5000 down to 2.4%.

The expense ratio of the average fund, that is the average amount of expenses that a fund charges its shareholders every year, was about 1.3% during the period. (Over the last couple of years expense ratios have been rising further and currently stand at 1.5%.) By comparison, the Vanguard S&P 500 expense ratio is 0.19%. Many funds also buy and sell their holdings at a rapid pace. Currently this turnover occurs at an average rate of 85% per year. This means that at the end of every year the average mutual fund only owns 15% of the same shares with which it started the year. The transaction costs involved in buying and selling so many shares every year result in an additional 0.7% of return disappearing every year.

Additionally, fund managers, believing that they can time the market, hold an average of about 8% of their portfolios in cash reserves. This practice has been a very expensive penalty during the bull market of the 1990s. This holding of cash reserves essentially explains the rest of the differential between mutual funds and the market. If you are invested in any mutual fund and are not currently aware of how expense ratios, turnover, market sector, and cash reserves apply to your fund, you are investing blind.

S&P index funds have garnered a lot of attention over the last couple of years for good reason. The Vanguard S&P 500 fund has outperformed over 90% of all domestic equity mutual funds over the past three and five years (and a much higher number if you include bond and international equity funds). But S&P index funds certainly aren't the only index funds—and in fact may not even be the best.

HOW WELL HAS ACTIVE PORTFOLIO MANAGEMENT WORKED LATELY?

The earlier documentation outlined in this book summarizes the futility, in the past, of attempting to outperform stock markets via active portfolio management. We might then be interested in just how well active portfolio management has done recently, compared to index-based investment.

As the following recent article from the *New York Times* details, superior portfolio returns using active portfolio management have been just as elusive over the past five years as previously. Most actively managed funds lagged market averages, and the best performance for all actively managed funds in the past five years surpassed market averages by only 3.6% per year. This record compares to a record of 6.2% per year outperformance, compared to the S&P 500 Average, for the approach to index-based investment (the System) described in this book, over the past 14 years.

Beating the Market: It's Still a Tall Order

Mark Hulbert

The New York Times

January 9, 2010

Trying to beat the market by buying and selling actively managed stock mutual funds?

You may want to reconsider. Model portfolios recommended by investment advisory newsletters regularly try to perform this trick, but generally fail. Even those that managed to make money during the recent bear market had trouble outperforming a simple stock index fund over an only moderately longer period: the last five years.

That is the finding of a study of nearly 200 model mutual fund portfolios by The Hulbert Financial Digest. These hypothetical portfolios, set up by editors of investment newsletters, used a combination of market timing and sector- and fund-rotation techniques to decide which funds to buy and sell, as well as when to do so. The study took into account redemption fees and front-end loads, or sales charges, as well as the penalties that fund companies sometimes assess for short-term trades.

Consider the model mutual fund portfolio that, of the 200 tracked, made the most money during the bear market of 2007-9: the "Rydex switchers portfolio" of Peter Eliades' *Stockmarket Cycles* newsletter. The strategy embodied in the portfolio called for more than two dozen transactions in the Rydex family of mutual funds over those 17 months. One fund that was bought and sold on several of those occasions was the Rydex Inverse S.& P. 500 2X Strategyfund, which is meant to double the performance of the Standard & Poor's 500-stock index, in the opposite direction.

Mr. Eliades's model portfolio gained 75 percent during that time—from October 2007 through February 2009—versus a 50 percent loss for an index fund benchmarked to the broad stock market, like the Vanguard Total Stock Market Index fund. As a result, the strategy beat a buy-and-hold approach by 125 percentage points.

Despite that enormous margin, the portfolio lagged behind the index fund over the five years through December—losing 0.8 percent, annualized, versus a positive return of 0.9 percent for the index fund.

The model portfolio's erratic performance, of course, constitutes just one example—but was nevertheless more the rule than the exception. It was one of 11 model mutual fund portfolios, of the 200 studied, that actually made money during the recent bear market. Over the five years through December, however, those 11 portfolios gained an average of just 1 percent, annualized.

During the same period, the average actively managed domestic equity fund tracked by Morningstar had a gain of 0.9 percent, annualized, matching the return of the index fund. Those results are statistically indistinguishable from the 1 percent average annualized five-year gain of those 11 newsletter portfolios.

(The best five-year performance, at 4.5 percent, annualized, was registered by the ProFunds/Rydex Sector Rotation Model Portfolio of the *Sector Navigator* newsletter.)

Why did the model portfolios that did well in the bear market have mediocre longer-term returns? One factor is that many of the advisers who manage them have been predominantly bearish for a number of years, not just during the bear market. Their model portfolios therefore lagged behind a buy-and-hold approach when the market started rising again. From the beginning of March through December, for example, the

11 model portfolios lost 5.1 percent, on average, versus a 56 percent gain for the Vanguard index fund.

Note that, over the last five years, portfolios that made money during the bear market fared no better, on average, than those at the opposite end of the spectrum: the portfolios that actually lost more than the market itself from the October 2007 high to the March 2009 low.

One lesson is that performance during a bear market has little to do with long-term returns. Both the best and the worst bear-market portfolios had difficulty beating a buy-and-hold approach over the longer term.

In an interview, Russell Wermers, a finance professor at the Smith School of the University of Maryland, said he has found from years of research that the odds of outperforming the market are very low, even for sophisticated professional money managers using the most advanced techniques. The odds are even worse for individual investors.

Professor Wermers acknowledged that the prospect of beating the market remains a powerful temptation for many people. But the recent bear market may have opened some investors' eyes, he said.

"If active management doesn't acquit itself in a five-year period that includes the worst bear market since the Depression," he said, "then it's yet more compelling evidence that most investors should not even try."

STOCK MARKET INVESTING: (F)UTILITY OF THE ADVICE OF STOCK ANALYSTS

It really is quite difficult to see how one can expect to invest successfully in individual stocks without very good advice, or at least good information. Although a great deal of data and analysis of individual stocks is available today, online and otherwise, the utility of the information is very questionable.

The recent *New York Times* article to follow documents the consistent tendency of stock analysts to recommend buying and holding the large majority of all stocks, but rarely to suggest selling. We are reminded of the situation in Lake Wobegon where "all the children are above average." This should lead us to wonder if analysts' recommendations are of any value; the monitoring of buy/sell decisions is not aided by published analyses since we can see that there is a consistent "buy" bias, but very little indication of when to sell. The evidence suggests that the ability to select promising stocks for purchase based on analysts' recommendations is very doubtful.

Why Analysts Keep Telling Investors to Buy

Jack Healy and Michael M. Grynbaum

The *New York Times*

February 9, 2009

Even now, with the recession deepening and markets on edge, Wall Street analysts say it is a good time to buy . . . Still.

At the top of the market, they urged investors to buy or hold onto stocks about 95 percent of the time. When stocks stumbled, they stayed optimistic. Even in November, when credit froze, the economy stalled and financial markets tumbled to their lowest levels in a decade, analysts as a group rarely said sell. And last month, as the Dow and Standard & Poor's 500-stock index suffered their worst January ever, analysts put a sell rating on a mere 5.9 percent of stocks, according to Bloomberg data. Many companies have taken such a beating in the downturn, analysts argue, that their shares are bound to bounce back.

Maybe. But after so many bad calls on so many companies, why should investors believe them this time? When Internet stocks imploded in 2000 and 2001, Wall Street analysts were widely scorned for fanning a frenzy that had inflated dot-com shares to unsustainable heights. But this time around, credit rating agencies, mortgage companies and Wall Street bankers have shouldered much of the blame for the Crash of 2008, and few have publicly questioned the analysts who urged investors to buy all the way down.

"Analysts completely missed the boat again with the subprime and credit crises," said Jacob Zamansky, a securities lawyer who represents investors. "They should've given some early warning signs to investors to bail out, or at least lighten up their portfolios. That warning never came."

Instead, many recommendations urged investors to hold on to their shares, or double down, as the bloodletting worsened.

On Oct. 8, as Congress and the Treasury Department frantically tried to calm the plummeting markets, a Citigroup analyst upgraded Bank of America to buy. Since then, Bank of America shares have fallen 77 percent. That same month, Jeffrey Harte, a top-rated analyst at Sandler O'Neill and Partners, also lifted Bank of America to buy, from hold, and a month later, he gave Citigroup the same upgrade, according to Bloomberg data. "Our ratings are based on 12-month price targets," Mr. Harte said. "Given the nature of economic cycles and, really, the focus of the new administration, I did expect and still do expect that the sector will improve considerably over the long term." With every wrenching decline, stocks seemed to be only better and better bargains to the most bullish market watchers, and their buy ratings seemed to reflect a hope that the market would soon turn a corner.

One analyst at Davenport & Company called the aluminum maker Alcoa a strong buy on March 24, Bloomberg data shows, when its stock was a buoyant $35 a share and commodities prices were rising. He then affirmed the rating 13 times as metals prices plunged, manufacturing dried up and Alcoa shares fell more than 70 percent.

"You can look back and say you were wrong as you go back and try to do a post-mortem on things," said John Rogers, director of research at the market research firm D. A. Davidson & Company. "I don't think there's ever 100 percent accurate predictive expertise. I wish there was." In July, Mr. Rogers put a buy rating on Chicago Bridge and Iron, an engineering and construction company whose stock fell sharply during the first half of 2008. The rebound Mr. Rogers hoped for never came: the stock plunged 65 percent more. Mr. Rogers said he did not expect oil prices, then hovering near $145 a barrel, to dwindle to $40. He did not expect

Chicago Bridge and Iron to hit snags on British natural gas developments. And he did not expect such a broad economic downturn. "If I had a rewind button and I could have done it, I would have downgraded on the day it peaked," he said. "I was wrong on that, and I think any analyst would have to acknowledge that."

In their defense, analysts point out that most regulators, economists, journalists and investors failed to foresee this financial catastrophe. And the worsening economy did prompt a cut in their buy recommendations. Investors, for their part, may have simply been following the lesson that had been beaten into them time and again during the bull years of the last decade: buy cheap because the market will always go up. "The market went up, up, up and up. You were rewarded for saying, 'Don't worry, be happy,'" said William A. Fleckenstein, president of Fleckenstein Capital, a money management firm in Issaquah, Wash. "Each time the market went down was a new opportunity to buy the stock even cheaper."

When the storms of last year hit, few investors realized that this pattern would suddenly vanish, with disastrous results. "They didn't understand the world they were operating in every year was a false reference point," Mr. Fleckenstein said. Still, the optimistic adage holds: the greater the fall, the greater the upside. Just give it some more time.

"Any analyst with a buy rating looks bad in a bear market," said Anthony Polini, an analyst at Raymond James who rates banks. "This group is dramatically oversold. It's down 75 percent. If you don't have some strong buy ratings at this point, you're doing a disservice to your customers." Mr. Polini, who has a strong buy rating on Bank of America, said it was a mistake to cut long-term outlooks for companies just because their stock price fell.

The actual investment recommendations coming from a sales desk can tell a different story from analysts' publicly released research. To gauge what clients are actually hearing from their investment managers, the investment-tracking firm First Coverage collects buy and sell recommendations from about 1,000 analysts that serve independent and midsize firms. At the end of January, 34.5 percent of the recommendations seen by First Coverage were for a sell or short call. That was up from 24 percent in December 2007. At the height of the market crash, in October and November, the proportion of sell calls reached about 45 percent. In all of 2008, sells never outweighed the buys.

Why, even amid cascading losses, could not the majority of analysts simply slash a company's rating to sell and tell investors to cut their losses?

"It doesn't matter if you're in a bear market, a bull market, a flat market, you're going to get 95 percent of the research coming out telling you to buy," said Randy Cass, chief executive of First Coverage. "It's just the way it's always been."

Although reforms after the dot-com bubble sought to make analysis more independent by separating it from investment banking, the broader culture on Wall Street still favors bulls. Some attribute the surplus of optimism to a widespread expectation that stocks—like home prices—will always increase in value over time. After all, the S.& P. 500 has posted annual returns of more than 9 percent during the last 80 years. Analysts did not want to hit the sell button just as the markets bottomed out.

HORSEMEN OF THE APOCALYPSE: HIGH FEES AND ADVISORS

As reviewed in Chapter 5, fees charged by advisors and others can have very serious long-term negative consequences for our real rates of return. The very high mutual fund fees charged in Canada are described in the article below.

It is difficult to imagine how these funds can justify charging such high fees, often in excess of 2%, if investors become aware of their consequences and begin to demand a more reasonable price/performance ratio. The possibility that ETFs may provide the competition essential to lowering these fees is discussed in this article.

Sky-High Fund Fees Finally Slipping

RBC Asset Follows TD, CI in Reducing Mutual Fund Costs

Jonathan Chevreau

Financial Post

April 13, 2007

Canada's world-beating mutual fund fees are finally starting to fall. Whether because of growing competition from low-cost exchange-traded funds (ETFs) or heightened consumer awareness, Canada's big banks are leading the charge. This week, RBC Asset Management Inc. announced cuts to management expense ratios (MERs) that Morningstar Canada says range from "significant" to "inconsequential." RBC president Brenda Vince says more than 80% of RBC funds will have lower MERs this year. The rest will stand pat, although a few F series funds may see minor MER increases, she says. The move follows an earlier 15 basis point (0.15%) cut to the "M" (management fee) portion of its MERs in January on several foreign equity funds. Now the second shoe has fallen: Effective July 1, RBC is dropping fees on the "ER" or expense ratio part of the equation on some international funds. Cuts to domestic funds are less dramatic.

As a research report by BMO Capital Markets' John Reucassell notes, "this action is similar to the steps taken by C.I. two years ago to fix the 'ER' portion in its mutual funds."

The two moves add up to "significant" cuts for RBC's foreign sector funds, says Rudy Luukko, investment funds editor for Morningstar Canada. Thus, RBC Global Consumer & Financial Fund, RBC Global Health Sciences and Global Technology fund all move from 2.75% to 2.18%. It's not clear if RBC's action, which follows similar earlier MER cuts by TD Mutual Funds, is a reaction to a controversial academic study that drew widespread media attention in 2006. In it, three professors (including one from Harvard) found Canada's MERs were higher than 18 other countries. Windsor, Ont.–based fund analyst Dan Hallett dismisses the study's impact. "Even if it was complete and not so deeply flawed, I doubt any firm would lower fees just because non-competing global peers are cheaper."

Long before that study, C.I. Funds dropped fees shortly after acquiring Assante Corp., one of the highest-MER shops in Canada. Bill Holland, chief executive officer of C.I. Financial, says MER cuts and greater transparency are both "inevitable" for the industry.

Oddly, given how competitive the business is, none of C.I's major competitors in the broker/dealer channel have yet matched C.I.'s MER cuts.

Morningstar's Luukko says "C.I. has nudged them down and in its segment it's been one of the major competitors that has been making moves to compete on costs as well as on investment management and other aspects. That's not been the case for some other prominent firms, such as AGF and Dynamic," Luukko says. Asked about this, Dynamic said it has reduced fees on more than 30 funds in the past three years. Holland admits ETFs are creating some pricing pressure. "Part of it for sure is ETFs," he said yesterday. "I think the banks want 100% market share so have moved fees down a bit. It's the dawn of a new level of competition."

The fund industry always claims MERs will fall as assets grow. However, this "economies of scale" argument doesn't appear to hold water. Luukko points out the three biggest RBC funds received MER cuts of zero, zero and one basis point this week. (A basis point is 0.01%). Luukko points to the largest fund in the country: the $13.6-billion Investors Dividend Fund. It has a 2.71% MER, far higher than the category median of 2.37% or the new 1.72% MER of the $8.7-billion RBC Canadian Dividend Fund. The latter's MER is cut only 1 basis point because RBC already considered it cost-competitive, Vince said. Dan Hallett attributes RBC's action to a "realization that fees are an issue; a point of differentiation and competitiveness in this industry." Capital International and Northwest have also reduced fees recently and "there are probably more to come," Hallett said. It's about time.

MORE FOOD FOR THOUGHT ON ADVISORS FROM AN EX-BROKER

The article is from a recent edition of the *Toronto Globe and Mail*, appearing in a section discussing retirement investing. It is based on the experience and opinions of a retired broker. He points out the lack of alignment, and in fact the conflict, between the goals of the individual investor and advisors in many cases, as described in Chapter 5. The broker, Garth Rustand, describes an organization he has founded, Investors Aid Co-operative of Canada (http://www.investors-aid.coop), which is attempting to provide investors with the information they need, free of the influence of fees and commissions on the advisor/broker. The philosophy seems similar to that of NAPFA (http://www.napfa.org), the National Association of Personal Financial Advisors in the U.S., described earlier.

What Can an Ex-Broker Teach You? Plenty

John Heinzl

The *Toronto Globe and Mail*

October 20, 2009

Nanaimo, B.C.'s Garth Rustand, founder of Investors-Aid Co-operative of Canada, used to be a successful broker Deddeda Stemler for the Globe And Mail.

For nearly 15 years, Garth Rustand worked as a stock broker with a big firm in Vancouver, pulling down $125,000 annually and being wined and dined by mutual fund companies pushing their latest offerings.

But as the money poured in, generated by fat commissions on funds and insurance products, he came to an uncomfortable realization: He was doing a lot better than the clients he was supposed to be helping.

"If you're on commission, it's very, very difficult, almost impossible, to do what's best for the client," says Mr. Rustand, 55. "You're being paid to generate commission, period." The problem with most adviser-client relationships is that the parties' interests aren't aligned, he says. The adviser is under pressure to sell expensive funds, wrap accounts and other products that generate the highest fees, but those high costs erode the client's returns.

Worse, many of the highest-commission products are the riskiest, exposing the client to potential losses.

The industry is built on "a huge conflict of interest," he says. Sadly, most consumers aren't aware of the conflicts when they turn their money over to an adviser whom they trust to do the right thing.

So in 2002, after his clients' nest eggs—and his conscience—suffered a blow in the tech meltdown, he decided to get out. He sold his "book" and started looking for ways to put his investment knowledge to better use.

"I wasn't feeling great about being a broker," he says.

Advisers behaving badly

Any of the following can be signs of a potentially problematic adviser, says the Investors-Aid Co-operative of Canada:

- *Frequent recommendations to trade*

  A well-built portfolio doesn't need a lot of changes. Excessive trading lines the adviser's pockets, not yours.
- *Pressure to invest in new products*

  Most packaged or hybrid products are expensive, complex, add little value and have low returns.
- *Dropping hints about a stock that's about to go up*

  This could be an enticement to trade stock, or an indication of insider trading.
- *No return calculations*

  The adviser may be trying to hide lousy returns.
- *Constant contact*

  Although everybody likes attention, too much can signal that your adviser is trying to generate fees. A good portfolio should be reviewed once a year or every six months at most.
- *No contact*

  The other extreme is when an adviser ignores you. Make sure you are getting the attention you need.

After a stint working for an ethical funds company, he began laying the groundwork for the Investors-Aid Co-operative of Canada. Launched in 2008, Investors-Aid is an independent organization owned by its 200-plus members. Its mission is to provide consumers with unbiased educational materials, online tools and investment advice.

THE "STUDY OF THE DECADE"

The following is a summary of a very interesting article published by Oxford University Press, and written by Daniel Bergstresser of Harvard Business School, John Chalmers of the University of Oregon, and Peter Tufano of Harvard Business School . The work describes a rather exhaustive study of the rates of return of investors who use advisors of various types to guide their mutual fund investments, and those who select and purchase mutual funds on their own. A communication summarizing the study (described as "The study of the decade") was written by Daniel Moine, in a publication of Morningstar, which is likely the leading U.S. publication evaluating and rating mutual funds.

The article provides some rather unexpected conclusions. Likely the most startling conclusion is that the independent investors attained a rate of return, during the study period from 1996 to 2002, which was more than twice that of those investors who relied on the guidance of advisors. While this result may certainly seem counterintuitive, it seems clear that there are many plausible factors accounting for this result. A very important reason for this unexpected finding seems to be that the primary motivation of many advisors may be their tendency, conscious or not, to maximize their own revenues rather than their clients'.

Mr. Moine notes that the authors of the scholarly article are not "anti-advisor," and this is an important point. Although I have been critical of stock analysts, advisors, brokers etc. in this book, I don't feel I am simply stating a case in opposition to such professionals. What I hope I am doing is making a case that such individuals have a responsibility to really provide a useful service to an investing public, which clearly is in need of high quality information and guidance. It seems more appropriate be "pro" advisors, analysts etc. who are truly effective, providing truly useful services which are very much needed in the present day.

The Study of the Decade

Donald Moine

June 26, 2006

http://trendfollowing.com/whitepaper/The%20Study%20of%20the%20Decade.pdf

"Assessing the Costs and Benefits of Brokers in the Mutual Fund Industry" is written by Daniel Bergstresser of Harvard Business School, John Chalmers of the University of Oregon, and Peter Tufano of Harvard Business School. While I earned my Ph.D. at the University of Oregon, I have no connection with Chalmers or the other authors. It is likely that this landmark work will soon become known as the "BCT Study" just as we all refer to the seminal work on asset allocation as the BHB study after the initials of its authors.

The BCT study is an exhaustive analysis of the cost and performance of more than 4,000 mutual funds sold by financial advisors and selected by investors on their own over the years 1996 to 2002. The amount of data analyzed is staggering. The study has been going on for years and various working drafts of the research findings are available on the Internet. The latest is dated Jan. 16, 2006.

The Findings

First of all, I must explain the usage of the word "broker" in the title of this study. It does not just apply to Series 7 licensed reps who work on commissions and loads. It truly applies to almost all financial advisors who sell mutual funds. The authors use the term "direct channel" to refer to what we might call "the public" or "do-it-yourselfers." This includes investors who buy mutual funds directly, on their own, or through no-load fund supermarkets.

All other mutual funds that are sold through banks, advice givers, RIAs, IARs, broker-dealers, mutual fund wrap accounts, wire houses and captive agents are included in the author's "broker channel." Unless you work for a fund supermarket on a salary, you are referred to as a "broker" in this study. In short, the authors' findings probably apply to the vast majority of all financial advisors, whether they are RIAs, IARs or registered representatives. This is the first study ever to scientifically quantify the benefits that investors may enjoy if they work with financial advisors. The authors asked these essential questions:

1. Do advisors give clients access to funds that are harder to find and evaluate? The answer is yes, but as you will see, as a whole, advisor-selected funds underperform funds that investors select on their own.

2. Do advisors help clients find funds that are lower cost (excluding distribution costs)? After analyzing several trillion dollars worth of transactions, the answer is no.

3. Do advisors give clients access to funds with better performance? The answer is a resounding no. I know this is shocking—and it may not apply to you. But the scientific evidence shows that many of the other advisors in America not only underperform indexes—they underperform what most people do on their own if they don't have an advisor.

4. Do advisors provide superior asset allocation? After years of research covering trillions of dollars of asset allocations, the finding is that advisors do not provide superior asset allocation. Even without this study, one only had to look at how advisors overemphasized technology funds in the late 1990s and how many advisors are overemphasizing energy, gold, and foreign funds today.

5. Do advisors help correct bad investor behavior such as chasing fads and chasing performance? The sobering answer is no. In fact, the evidence shows that advisors even contribute to such behavior. Again, look at all the money advisors are pouring into energy, gold, and foreign funds.

It is important to note that the authors are not anti-advisor. Remarkably, they had the cooperation and support of some of the largest and most respected industry groups and research organizations in America in working on this study. Further, the authors go out of their way to point out that financial advisors may offer significant "intangible benefits."

Unfortunately, these researchers found that the clients of advisors buy funds that have substantially higher fees and lower risk-adjusted returns than funds that investors buy on their own. The implications of these findings are staggering.

For much too long, some advisors have been engaging in investment practices that provide minimal or non-existent benefit to clients. For example, the BCT study found that the raw returns of equally weighted mutual funds (net of all expenses) for 1996 to 2002 were 6.626% for the investors working on their own and were 2.924% for funds provided by advisors.

In other words, the public working on its own did more than 100% better than financial advisors when it came to selecting equity mutual funds. After factoring in inflation and taxes, clients of financial advisors lost money and lost purchasing power. This must change.

RISK MANAGEMENT: RECENT EXPERIENCE WITH ASSET DIVERSIFICATION

The *Economist* magazine discusses asset diversification into a wide range of vehicles, including those beyond standard stock and bond investing, over the past year. In general, such diversification has not been effective in improving returns, since all asset classes have endured similar drops in value. While diversification is clearly a bedrock investment principle, it does appear to have definite limitations.

All Bets Are Off

Spreading the Risk has Spread the Losses

The *Economist*

Oct 30, 2008

There is such a thing as a free lunch. That, at least, is what pension funds have been told in recent years. Diversify into new asset classes and your portfolio can improve the trade-off between risk and return because you will be making uncorrelated bets. Boy, did pension funds diversify. They bought emerging-market equities, corporate bonds, commodities and property, while giving money to hedge funds and private-equity managers with their complex strategies and high fees. The idea was to "be like Yale," the university endowment fund run by David Swensen, a celebrated investor, which started to diversify into hedge funds and private equity in the 1980s. Compared with other institutional investors over the past 20 years, Yale had very little exposure to conventional equities. It also produced remarkably strong returns.

But those who thought Yale had found the key to success have been disappointed. Every one of those diversified bets has turned sour this year. In retrospect, it looks like the strategy had two problems. The first was that all risky assets were boosted by the same factors: low interest rates and healthy global growth. That encouraged investors to use leverage, or borrowed money, to enhance returns. The result was what Jeremy Grantham of GMO, a fund-management group, describes as "the first truly global bubble." As confidence has unraveled, investors have been forced to sell all those asset classes simultaneously, driving down prices across the board. The second, and related, problem is that some of the asset classes were quite small. Initially, this illiquidity was attractive since it seemed to offer more alluring returns. And as more investors became involved, their liquidity duly improved. But they still suffer from the "rowing boat" factor. When everyone tries to exit the asset class at once, the vessel capsizes.

Furthermore, some of these asset classes were always likely to be driven by the same factors as stock markets. Private-equity funds, for example, give investors exposure to the same kinds of risks as quoted companies, only with added leverage. So was the whole idea of diversification a write-off from the start? The strategy's defenders say no. They argue that pension funds (and other institutional investors) had made too big a bet on equities in the 1990s. When the bet went wrong with the bursting of the dotcom bubble, funds went into deficit. They accept that, in a crisis, correlations head towards one; in other words, all asset classes (except government bonds) tend to fall together. But the diversifiers have three counter-arguments.

The first is that any correlation less than one is still worth having. Hedge funds may have performed badly this year but their losses have been far lower than those of equity markets. Second, there is a difference between short-term correlations and long-term ones. If you take a five- or ten-year view, it still looks as if property, commodities and the rest offer some diversification benefits. They did so during the equity bear market of 2000-02, for example. Third, consultants like Colin Robertson of Hewitt Associates argue that diversification does work when it is applied in a sophisticated way. There is no point in diversifying if the investment does not offer a genuinely different source of return (much of private equity falls into this category) or if the asset is already overvalued.

Yet even allowing for this, diversification has surely not offered the benefits most pension funds expected. Indeed, it may have had perverse results. In the old days, with equities trading at below-average valuations, funds would now be on a buying spree. They could afford to ignore the short-term risks because of the long-term nature of their liabilities. Pension funds thus acted as an automatic stabiliser for the market. This time round, that does not seem to be happening. One reason may be accounting changes which make pension-fund managers more focused on the short term. Another, however, may be the strategic drive to diversification. The *Wall Street Journal* has reported that CalPERS, America's largest public-pension fund, has been selling shares to meet commitments to put more money into private-equity firms.

The final problem with diversification has been the cost. Investing in quoted shares via an index fund is very cheap—a fraction of a percentage point. But diversified asset classes cost more to trade and involve higher management fees, expenses that eat into pension-fund returns. So perhaps diversification has been a free lunch after all. Not for the pension funds, but for the fund managers.

USING THE PAST TO TRY TO MAKE SOME SENSE OF THE FUTURE

Those who believe we should learn from history, since we are likely to repeat it, should pay close attention to the next contribution from the *New York Times,* published during the market meltdown in the fall of 2008. The article, by David Leonhardt, investigates the current valuation of U.S. markets following some significant declines, and finds that stocks are not really undervalued by historical standards. The question then is will they fall still further as the economy continues to deteriorate?

Are Stocks the Bargain You Think?

David Leonhardt

The *New York Times*

October 29, 2008

Some of the country's most famous investors, including Warren Buffett and John Bogle, have started to make the case that it's time to dive back into the stock market. They are usually careful to add that they don't know what stocks will do in the short term. Yet their basic message is clear enough: stocks are now cheap, irrational fears have been driving the market down lately, and people who buy today will be glad that they did. After a day like Tuesday, when the market rose 11 percent, it's easy to see the merits of the argument.

But there is another argument that deserves more attention than it has gotten so far. It's the bearish argument that is based neither on fears that the country may be sliding into another depression nor on gut-level worries about the unknown. It is based on numbers and history, and it has at least as much claim on reason as the bullish argument does. It goes something like this: Stocks are truly cheap only relative to their values over the last 20 years, a period that will go down as one of the great bubbles in history. If you take a longer view, you see that the ratio of stock prices to corporate earnings is only slightly below its long-term average. And in past economic crises—during the 1930s and 1970s—stocks fell well below their long-run average before they turned around. To make matters worse, corporate earnings have now started to plunge, too. Assuming that they keep dropping, stocks would also need to fall to keep the price-earnings ratio at its current level.

As stocks were soaring on Tuesday afternoon, I called James Melcher to hear a dose of fact-based bearishness. Mr. Melcher is president of Balestra Capital, a hedge fund in New York, who wrote an essay for his clients two years ago that predicted the broad outlines of the financial crisis (and then arranged Balestra's portfolio accordingly). Like the bulls, he said that no one could know what the market would do in the short term. "But to think stocks are cheap now," he added, "is not rational." He went on: "In the last 20 years—and particularly in the last six or seven—you had the most massive creation of liquidity the world has ever known." Consumers went ever deeper into debt, thanks to loose lending standards, and a shadow banking system, made up of hedge funds and investment banks, allowed Wall Street to do the same. All that debt lifted economic growth and stock returns. "It was a nice party," Mr. Melcher said. "The problem is that all the bills are coming due at the same time." He thinks stocks could easily fall an additional 20 percent and maybe 35 percent before hitting bottom.

So who's right—the bears or the bulls? The smartest people in both camps, like Mr. Melcher, Mr. Buffett and Mr. Bogle, have a healthy dose of humility about their own conclusions. And when you dig into their arguments, you find that they're not quite as different as they first sound. But they are different, and it's worth taking a minute to consider the numbers. There are any number of ways to measure the valuation of the stock market. Some examine prices relative to earnings, others are based on cash flow, a company's underlying assets or the total value of the market. But they tell a pretty consistent story right now. Stocks, which were fabulously expensive for much of the 1990s and this decade, no longer are.

My favorite measure is the one recommended by Benjamin Graham and David L. Dodd, in their classic 1934 textbook, Security Analysis. They urged investors to use a price-to-earnings ratio—stock prices divided by average annual corporate earnings—based on at least five years of earnings and, ideally, closer to 10. Corporate profits may rise or fall in any given year, but a share of stock is a claim on a company's long-term earnings and should be evaluated as such. (Why not use a forecast of future earnings? Because they tend toward the fictional, as we're now seeing once again.)

The 10-year price-to-earnings ratio tells an incredibly consistent story over the last century. It has averaged about 16 over that time. There have been long periods when it stayed above 16 and even shot above 20, like the 1920s, 1960s and recent years. As recently as last October, when other measures suggested the market was reasonably valued, the Graham-Dodd version of the ratio was a disturbing 27. But periods in which the ratio has jumped above 20 have always been followed by steep declines and at least a decade of poor returns. By 1932, the ratio had fallen to 6. In 1982, it was only 7. Then, of course, the market began to self-correct in the other direction, and stocks took off. After Tuesday's big rally, the ratio was just a shade below 16, or almost equal to its long-run average. This is a little difficult to swallow, I realize. Stocks are down 40 percent since last October, and every experience from the last 25 years suggests they now have to bounce back.

But that's precisely the problem. Since the 1980s, stocks have always bounced back from a loss, usually reaching a high in relatively short order. As a result, the market became enormously overvalued. As Robert Shiller, the economist who specializes in bubbles, points out, human beings tend to put too much weight on recent experiences. We think the market snapbacks of 1987 and the current decade are more meaningful and more predictive than the long slumps of the 1930s, 1940s and 1970s. Of course, anyone who made the same assumption in 1930 or 1975—this just has to turn around soon—would have had to wait years and years until the investment paid off. Now, Mr. Buffett, Mr. Bogle and their fellow bulls know all this history, and they're still bullish. (Though I'd be more bullish, too, if I could get the favorable terms that Mr. Buffett did. In exchange for his money and his good name, Goldman Sachs and General Electric each guaranteed him an annual return of at least 10 percent.)

So on Tuesday afternoon, I also called Mr. Bogle, the legendary founder of the Vanguard Group, the investment firm whose low-cost index funds have made a lot for a lot of people. He, too, prefers the 10-year price-to-earnings ratio, he said, but he didn't think that it necessarily had to fall to the same bargain-basement levels it reached in the 1930s and 1970s. You can certainly see why that would be the case. Investors are well aware that the market fell to irrationally low levels during past crises, and they may not allow it to become so cheap this time around. Mr. Bogle also thinks that corporate profits will rebound nicely within a couple of years and likes the fact that interest rates are low. Low rates have often—though not always—accompanied bull markets.

But it was his last argument that I think is the main one for most investors to focus on. "I'm not looking for a great bull market," he said. There are some reasons to be optimistic about stocks, he said, "and I also look at the alternative." And, really, how attractive are the alternatives? Savings accounts and money market funds will struggle to keep pace with inflation. Bonds may, as well. Stocks, on the other hand, are paying an average dividend of about 3 percent, which is better than the interest on many savings accounts, and stocks are also almost certain to rise over the next couple of decades.

If that is your time frame—decades, rather than months or years—this will probably turn out to be a perfectly good buying opportunity. In the shorter term, though, it's a much tougher call, and it involves a lot more risk.

LIKELY FUTURE ECONOMIC SCENARIOS

Finally, while still remembering Galbraith's statement that the only function of economic forecasting is to make astrology look respectable, it seems a good idea to consider various future possibilities for the economy. We might want to become more aggressive investors, if we conclude that the end of the downturn is in sight, but not if continued turmoil seems in order. A continuation of market turbulence will likely limit the performance a pure buy-and-hold approach.

In this article from the *Wall Street Journal* by David Wessel, the most likely scenario is felt to be a "long slog," or a directionless economy in turmoil for a long time to come. The article doesn't really indicate just how long, however.As noted in chapter 14 bear cycles typically last about 16 or more years, so perhaps 8 or 10 more years of "slogging" may be in order.

Long Odds? Three Scenarios for the Economy's Path

David Wessel

The *Wall Street Journal*

April 23, 2009

There is no doubt where the economy is now. "By any measure, this downturn represents by far the deepest global recession since the Great Depression," the International Monetary Fund declared Wednesday.

But there's more than the usual uncertainty about where it is going. The key is the U.S. Even though its slice of the world economy is smaller than it once was, it's still huge. The U.S. led the world into the abyss, and it will lead the world economy out of it.

But how fast and when?

The alphabet can help to imagine the possibilities and the path of the economy. There's the letter V: the kind of quick rebound that usually follows a deep recession. Or U: a longer recession and slow recovery. There is L: years of painfully slow growth. And W: a temporary upturn as the economy feels the jolt of fiscal stimulus that quickly wears off. Finally, there's the big D, not the shape but another Great Depression.

With History a Guide, Consider Three Starkly Different Scenarios

THE V The late Victor Zarnowitz, a student of the business cycle, had a rule: "Deep recessions are almost always followed by steep recoveries." The mild recession of the early 1990s and early 2000s were followed by mild recoveries. But the U.S. economy grew faster than a 6% pace in the four quarters after the deep 1973–75 recession and faster than a 7.75% pace after the even deeper 1980–82 downturn.

The IMF says this is the worst recession that the world has seen since the Great Depression. So what will happen next? Economics Editor David Wessel discusses three possible scenarios.

"In deep recessions," says Michael Mussa of the Peterson Institute for International Economics, "there is usually a growing sense of gloom as the recession deepens." Then the forces that triggered recession—say, plunging home prices—abate. The adrenaline of tax cuts and government spending kicks in. With inventories so lean, the slightest uptick in demand prompts a sharp increase in production, and the natural dynamism of capitalism reasserts itself.

"Experience suggests all of this should work, and I believe it will," Mr. Mussa predicts. Governments have administered huge doses of fiscal and monetary stimulus. Home-building and car-buying are so low they can't fall much further. Many consumers shy away from buying because they're frightened, not broke, and that state of mind can change quickly and liberate pent-up demand.

But the Federal Reserve caused the deep recessions of the 1970s and 1980s when it put its foot on the brake to stop inflation; it ended them when it let up. This time, Fed has its foot to the floor and the economy is still slowing. And so much stock-market and housing wealth has evaporated that a quick turn in consumer spirits seems unlikely. Plus, the repair of the banks remains far from complete, restraining lending.

The odds of the V: 15%.

THE BIG D If one asked a roomful of economists two years ago to put odds on a repeat of the Great Depression, nearly all would have said zero. In early March, The Wall Street Journal posed the question to about 50 forecasters—defining depression as a decline in output per person of more than 10%, four times worse than the decline the IMF anticipates.

On average, they put odds at one in seven; several put them above one in four.

"This is a Depression-sized event," says economic historian Barry Eichengreen of the University of California at Berkeley, citing the global decline in industrial production and world trade. The big difference: In 1929, governments dithered, or worse. In 2009, they've rushed to the rescue.

To go from today's deep recession to a depression something would have to go wrong. It could be a financial catastrophe on the scale of last fall's bankruptcy by Lehman Brothers or another panic-inducing event. Or a crash in the dollar, one that forces interest rates up at just the wrong moment. Or it could be political gridlock that stops governments in the U.S. or Europe from spending enough to fix the banks before a big one fails, or keeps them for doing more on the fiscal or monetary fronts as the economy deteriorates.

Or it could be virulent deflation that pulls down prices and incomes, making debts, which don't fall when prices do, a heavier burden. The textbook remedy is easy money and big government deficits. But so much of that has been tried it's easy to question its efficacy or to imagine resistance around the world to doing.

The odds of the big D: 20%.

THE L For a decade after its stock market and real-estate bubble burst in 1990, Japan bumped along at an annual growth of just 0.5%. It was dubbed the Lost Decade, and it could happen here. The recession ends but the economy plods along, growing too slowly to bring down unemployment for years.

As the IMF observed this week, recoveries following recession caused by financial crises are "typically slower." Those following recessions that occur simultaneously across the globe "have typically been weak." Back in the 1990s, as U.S. banks struggled, the Fed talked a lot about "financial headwinds." Those were zephyrs compared to the gale-force winds that the economy confronts today.

If financial markets stabilize but don't improve steadily, or if housing prices continue to drift down, or if confidence remains shaky, the U.S. economy could languish for a time. American consumers, once known for spending in the face of prosperity or adversity, could finally decide to prepare for retirement by saving more, having just learned that neither 401(k) retirement accounts nor home values rise inexorably. And the U.S. can't count on increasing exports, the solution when emerging-market economies run into financial trouble and the reason Japan didn't do even worse in the 1990s. The rest of the world is in no shape to buy.

An unfolding depression could scare Congress to act boldly, but the L is less ominous—and perhaps more likely as a result. There would be months when the economy appeared to be strengthening so the temptation to wait-and-see would be strong.

Put the odds of the L at 55%. That adds to 90%. So put 10% odds on the U, less pleasant than the euphoric V but far less painful than a Lost Decade. That's the rough consensus of economic forecasters; it means U.S. unemployment grows for another year and a half.

Bottom line: The odds favor a long slog.

References

CHAPTER 1

1. Bernstein, W. 2002. *The Four Pillars of Investing*. New York: McGraw-Hill; Bogle, J. 1999. *Common Sense on Mutual Funds*. New York: John Wiley and Sons; Larimore, T., M. Lindauer, and M. LeBoeuf. 2006. *The Bogleheads Guide to Investing*. Hoboken: John Wiley and Sons.; Malkiel, B. 1996. *A Random Walk Down Wall Street*. New York: W. W. Norton.

CHAPTER 2

1. *Wikipedia*. "Wall $treet Week." http://en.wikipedia.org/wiki/Wall_$treet_Week.
2. Bernstein, W. 2002. *The Four Pillars of Investing*. New York: McGraw-Hill; Bogle, *Common Sense on Mutual Funds*; Malkiel, *A Random Walk Down Wall Street*.

CHAPTER 3

1. *New York Times*. "From Here to Retirement" (Editorial). January 25, 2009.
2. *History of 401(k) Plans: An Update*. Employee Benefit Research Institute, 2005.
3. Ibid.
4. Tergesen, A. "How to Fix 401(k)s." *Wall Street Journal*. December 14, 2008.
5. Bernard, T.S. "401(k)s: What You Need to Know." *New York Times*. December 26, 2008.
6. Smith, H. "Can You Afford to Retire?" *Frontline*. May 16, 2006.

7. Greene, K. Baby Boomers Delay Retirement. *Wall Street Journal.* September 22, 2008.
8. Tergesen, "How to Fix 401(k)s."
9. *Wall Street Journal.* "When 401(k) Investing Goes Bad." August 4, 2008; Bernard, "401(k)s: What You Need to Know."

CHAPTER 4

1. Jensen, M. 1967. "The Performance of Mutual Funds." *Journal of Finance* 23(2):389–416.
2. Ibid.
3. Gruber, M. 1996. "Another Puzzle: The Growth in Actively Managed Mutual Funds." *Journal of Finance.* July, LI(3):783–810.
4. Malkiel, *A Random Walk Down Wall Street.*
5. Bogle, *Common Sense on Mutual Funds.*
6. Ibid.
7. Bernstein, *The Four Pillars of Investing.*
8. Ibid.
9. Healy, J. and M.M. Grynbaum. "Why Analysts Keep Telling Investors to Buy." *New York Times.* February 9, 2009.
10. McLean, B. and P. Elkind. 2004. *The Smartest Guys in the Room: The Amazing Rise and Scandalous Fall of Enron.* New York: Penguin Group.
11. Buffet, M., and D. Clark. 1997. *Buffetology.* New York: Rawson Associates.
12. Graham, B. 1976. *Financial Analysts Journal.*
13. Malkiel, *A Random Walk Down Wall Street.*
14. Bogle, *Common Sense on Mutual Funds*; Bernstein, *The Four Pillars of Investing.*
15. Bernstein, *The Four Pillars of Investing.*
16. Gruber, "Another Puzzle."

CHAPTER 5:

1. Federation of Tax Administrators (http://www.taxadmin.org).
2. Goodman, P.S. "Deflation." *New York Times*. October 31, 2008; Reddy, S. "Amid Pressing Problems, Threat of Deflation Looms." *Wall Street Journal*. October 18, 2008.
3. *Wall Street Journal*, "When 401(k) Investing Goes Bad."
4. Ibid.
5. Ibid.
6. Smith, "Can You Afford to Retire?"
7. Schwed, F., Jr. 1940. *Where Are the Customers' Yachts?* New York: Simon & Schuster.
8. Chevreau, J. 2007. "Mutual Fund Fees Around the World." *Financial Post*. October 31, 2005.
9. Heinzl, J. "What can an Ex-Broker Teach You? Plenty." *Toronto Globe and Mail*. October 20, 2009.
10. Fairfield, H. "For a Retirement Plan, Stocks = Top Returns (Usually)." *New York Times*. October 19, 2008.
11. Moine, D. "The Study of the Decade." 2006. *Morningstar*. http://advisor.morningstar.com/articles.
12. Heinzl, "What can an Ex-Broker Teach You?"
13. Moine, "The Study of the Decade;" Heinzl, "What Can an Ex-Broker Teach You?"
14. Fulford, M. 2008. "Managing the Financial Services Industry Instead of Letting it Manage You." *Real World Personal Finance Software*.
15. {SEE PAGE 69. AU/ED PLEASE FILL IN}

CHAPTER 6

1. Graham, B. 1973. *The Intelligent Investor, Fifth Edition*. New York: Harper & Row.
2. Bogle, *Common Sense on Mutual Funds*.
3. Malkiel, *A Random Walk Down Wall Street*.
4. Bernstein, W. 2002. *The Four Pillars of Investing*. New York: McGraw-Hill.

CHAPTER 7

1. Bernstein, W. 2002. *The Four Pillars of Investing*, New York: McGraw-Hill.
2. Malkiel, B. 1996. *A Random Walk Down Wall Street.*
3. Wikipedia, Wall $treet Week.
4. Pring, M. 1980. *Technical Analysis Explained*. New York: McGraw-Hill.
5. Ibid.
6. Schannep, J. 2008. *Dow Theory for the 21st Century*. New York: John Wiley and Sons.
7. Zweig, M. 1986. *Winning on Wall Street*. New York: Warner Books.
8. Zweig, M. 1997. *Winning on Wall Street, Revised Edition*. New York: Warner Books.

CHAPTER 8

1. Bernstein, *The Four Pillars of Investing*; Bogle, *Common Sense on Mutual Funds*; Malkiel, *A Random Walk Down Wall Street.*
2. Bernstein, *The Four Pillars of Investing.*
3. Pring, *Technical Analysis Explained.*

CHAPTER 9

1. *CIA World Factbook*. 2008.
2. Ibid.
3. Ibid.

CHAPTER 10

1. Bernstein, *The Four Pillars of Investing*; Malkiel, *A Random Walk Down Wall Street.*
2. Pring, *Technical Analysis Explained.*
3. Zweig, *Winning on Wall Street*; Zweig, *Winning on Wall Street, Revised Edition*.
4. Bernstein, *The Four Pillars of Investing;* Bogle, *Common Sense on Mutual Funds.*
5. Bogle, *Common Sense on Mutual Funds.*

6. Bernstein, *The Four Pillars of Investing;* Bogle, *Common Sense on Mutual Funds.*
7. *CIA World Factbook.*

CHAPTER 11

1. Zweig, J. "What History Tells Us About the Market." *Wall Street Journal.* October 11, 2008.
2. Zweig, *Winning on Wall Street*; Zweig, *Winning on Wall Street, Revised Edition.*
3. Thorp, E. 1966. *Beat the Dealer: A Winning Strategy for the Game of Twenty-One.* New York: Vintage Books.

CHAPTER 12

1. Shiller, R. 2005. *Irrational Exuberance.* Princeton, NJ: Princeton University Press; Smith, M. 2003. *The Equity Culture: The Story of the Global Stock Market.* New York: Farrar, Straus and Giroux.

CHAPTER 14

1. Zweig, "What History Tells Us About the Market."
2. Shiller, R. 2005. *Irrational Exuberance.* Princeton, NJ: Princeton University Press.
3. Graham, *The Intelligent Investor, Fifth Edition.*
4. Leonhardt, D. "Are Stocks the Bargain You Think?" *New York Times.* October 29, 2008.
5. *Economist.* "The End of the Affair." November 20, 2008.
6. Ibid.

CHAPTER 15

1. Greenspan, S. "Why We Keep Falling for Financial Scams." *Wall Street Journal.* January 3, 2009.

Index

A

B

T

U

V

W

Z

Index by Nancy K. Humphreys, www.wordmapsindexing.com